THE BALISONG  L

by Jeff Imada
with George Foon

WARNING: The author and publisher are not responsible in any manner whatsoever for any injury which may occur by reading and/or following the instructions herein. Also, some states and governmental agencies have imposed legal limitations on the possession of certain weapons, so consult your local laws and regulations for any applicable restrictions.

ISBN: 0-86568-102-3

KNOW NOW PUBLISHING COMPANY
Distributed by: **Unique Publications**
4201 Vanowen Place, Burbank, CA 91505, (800) 332-3330

CONTENTS

DEDICATION

I dedicate this book first and foremost to my parents, Tad and Toshi Imada, who brought me into this world, taught me about living, and who've *always* given me their love and support.

Dan Inosanto who made the martial arts a part of my life by giving me the keys and concepts for physical, mental and spiritual growth.

My Jeet Kune Do and Kali/Escrima brothers and sisters on our mutual and separate journeys through life. May we grow strong together.

ACKNOWLEDGEMENTS

I'd like to thank my publisher, George Foon, for bringing it all together, Les and Roberta de Asis of Pacific Cutlery Corporation who wanted me to write this book four years ago, my brother and training partner, Brian Imada, and Chris Kent, my JKD brother, for contributing to the photo sessions.

FOREWORD

The knife and knife fighting are the backbones of the Filipino martial arts. The difference between life or death rests solely on your skill, so there is little wonder why the Filipino martial arts are so effective and popular today.

A product of that art is the unique and flashy Filipino balisong knife, which is currently sweeping the knife and martial arts world. After reading many articles about it—most with incorrect information—we at Know Now want to set the record straight with the true facts and history of this exciting weapon.

The knife, any knife, carries with it connotations of evil, blood and death, but in actuality the defeat of the Spanish Armada in 1588 gave final proof that hand weapons could no longer compete with gunpowder. In 1976 we were reluctant to reveal the dagger techniques in Dan Inosanto's FILIPINO MARTIAL ARTS book. But today with so many easier ways to inflict genocide, we can discuss the blade with a clear conscience. No knife can compete with a "Saturday night special," or with a sniper with a telescopic sight and a 1/16-inch trigger pull. As a famous historian aptly put it when referring to the invention of gunpowder, "Without it so many brave and valiant men would not have died at the hands of cowards. . . ."

Saturday night special: A cheap, small caliber handgun that is easily bought in a gun store or ordered by mail. Since a great many of these purchases were made to satisfy the passions of Saturday night, Detroit lawmen began referring to the weapons as "Saturday night specials."

ABOUT THE AUTHOR

Jeff Imada, though young in age and unobtrusive in nature, is one of the three leading exponents in popularizing the balisong knife.

First, he is a martial artist with 15 years of absorbing what is useful. He currently has the honor of being among an elite handful of individuals qualified as "certified JKD/Kali instructor" for the Dan Inosanto Academies. Jeff was indeed fortunate to have studied, traveled, demonstrated and made movies with Dan Inosanto since he first opened his academy's doors to the public following Bruce Lee's untimely passing.

Second, Jeff is the technical advisor to Pacific Cutlery, one of the world's most respected quality knife manufacturers. Pacific Cutlery Corporation is the only licensed manufacturer of the patented Bali-Song knife and the only registered owner of the name "Bali-Song."

Third, Jeff is the best-known "unknown" in the motion picture and television industry. He has appeared as technical advisor, stunt double and/or featured player in just about every prime-time television action series, including "Fall Guy," "The Incredible Hulk," "You Asked for It," "Massarati and the Brain," "Tales of the Gold Monkey," "Bring 'Em Back Alive," "Hart to Hart," "General Hospital," "Taxi," "A-Team," "Air Wolf," "Manimal," "The Master" and "T.J. Hooker," to name a few. Moreover, he was responsible for use of the balisong knife in "Nice Dreams," "Magnum P.I.," "Strike Force," and "Matt Houston," and got Dan Inosanto the villain's part in "Sharkey's Machine." Backed by top-quality, wide exposure, the balisong will undoubtedly rival the nunchaku in popularity for action film sequences.

This impressive background, plus the ownership of a balisong since his elementary school days, convinced us that Jeff was more than qualified to author our treatise. We asked Jeff how he felt about writing a book on knives and knife fighting. After some soul searching, he replied, "Dan [Inosanto] always stressed that to successfully defend against a knife, you must first *be* a knife fighter. I hope the readers will look at it from a moral/defensive point of view. After all, you don't buy fire insurance because you want your house to burn down, or life insurance because you *want* to die. No, you just want to be prepared in case the need arises."

The element of freedom while training with Dan Inosanto and his no limitation philosophy changed my life and gave me the courage to maybe one day write a book.

Traveling does broaden your scope and outlook. The president of Chile was really impressed with our Kali demonstration. I am thinking, "Imagine what he would have thought of all the things that Dan didn't show him."

This scene culminates a flashy opening display with the balisong in Cheech and Chong's "Nice Dreams."

I am stunt doubling for actor John Fujioka on the TV show, "Tales of the Gold Monkey." Can you tell us apart?

One of the fringe benefits in the entertainment business is getting to meet and work with stars like Heather Locklear, here on the set of "T.J. Hooker."

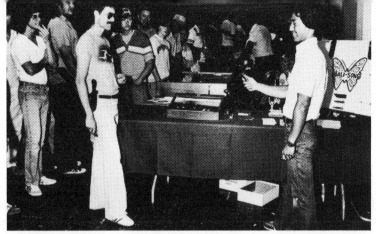

I am demonstrating how to manipulate the balisong at a knife show in Los Angeles. In the audience was Tony Bronson, son of Charles (far left) and noted author David E. Steele (foreground).

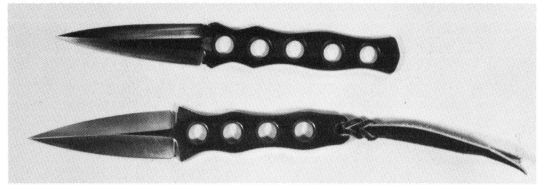

One of my duties as technical advisor for Pacific Cutlery involved testing their designs. The top model was the prototype for their SR-71 Sport/ Recreation/Survival/Rescue knife. My input (bottom) helped create a more contoured handle with a larger notched thumb and finger guard to prevent the hand from sliding onto the blade, along with a more tapered rear for a better palm fit. My Filipino martial arts knife training was invaluable for testing strokes, jabs, slashes, stabs, etc.

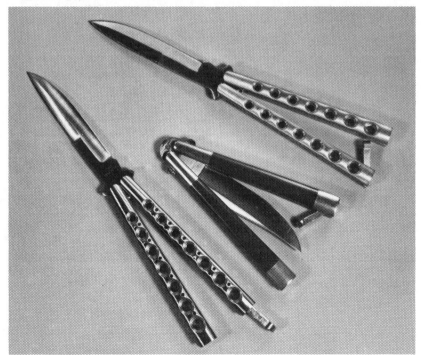

My suggestion for the balisong knife involves a more rigid latch. The center and top right photos show how it can get in the way during manipulation, as you will discover when you begin extensive manipulations with the knife.

HISTORY

The knife is one of the most ancient tools known to man. In its earliest form, it consisted of a piece of wood, stone or bone with a jagged edge. Human creativity soon led to chipping, rubbing or flaking the material to produce a crude cutting implement. This was the first product of human ingenuity dating back millions of years, and an act that led to man's dominance over animals.

The balisong, or Filipino butterfly knife, is one of the ancient weapons of Kali, the ancestral art of all the Malaya-Polynesian fighting systems. This mystic art is considered to be the deadliest fighting system in the world. Kali's domain was rooted in the Malay archipelago, but its scope of influence reached far beyond its territorial sphere. In some parts of the Orient, as well as Africa, the Pacific islands, Central and South America, Kali was and still is considered the art of arts.

The knife's ancestry dates back to the latter part of the T'ang dynasty, around 800 A.D. An ancient Filipino legend recalls the story of one warrior trained in the Filipino martial arts who dispatched 29 enemies with a folding knife. That knife, the forerunner of today's balisong, is referred to by native Filipinos as the "Veintinueve," which means 29 in memory of that feat.

The original knife took its name from a small barrio called Balisung, in the Batangas region of the Philippines. The people of that town are noted solely for producing this knife. According to the elders of that area, the art of making this particular knife has been handed down for centuries by their forefathers.

Literally translated, "bali" means to break, and "sung" means horn. The early handles were carved out of animal horns. This was the "broken horn knife."

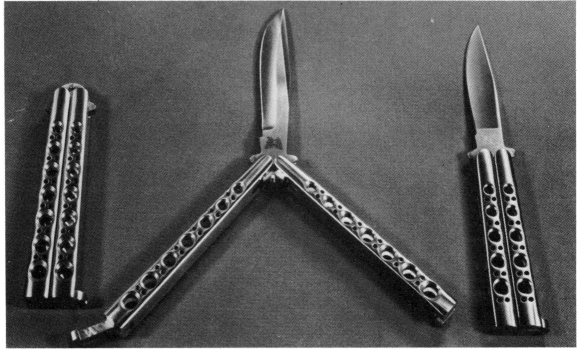

The balisong has many ancestral meanings. Fully closed, it symbolizes "3 in 1 for peace." Partially opened, it represents the three geographical locations of ancient forefathers. Fully opened, it signifies "3 in 1 for combat."

This hunting knife, imported from Finland, was a version of the balisong knife that was directly affected by the switchblade ban. It was made by Hackman and imported by the Garcia Corporation. In actuality, the plastic handles were too light to manipulate effectively.

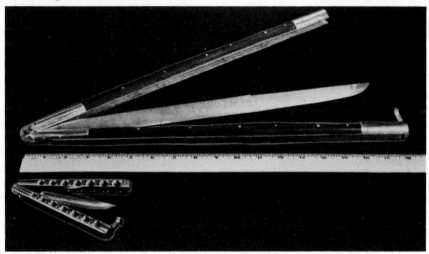

This was the famous "Veintinueve" or 29. It was jokingly said to be long enough to impale 29 men with one thrust. Coincidentally, the most powerful handgun in the world is also called the "29." It's the Smith & Wesson 29, the 44 magnum used by Clint Eastwood in his "Dirty Harry" films.

The early butterfly knives were made from available materials, and were rather crude when compared to Japanese blades. But unlike Japanese blades, the balisongs weren't meant to pierce through feudal armor. In the heat of the tropics, the target of a balisong was usually a nearly nude human body. For that purpose, they were more than adequate.

The first butterfly knives were introduced to the States by early Filipino immigrant farm laborers, and by returning GIs who brought them back as war souvenirs. The soldiers referred to them as "click-click" knives because of their fancy but noisy action. For the same reason, the Filipino-American kids of that era called them "bali-songs"—"bali" meaning to break and "song" for the song of the blade. In the Filipino communities like Stockton, California, the balisong was as common as baseball to American kids. Every 5-year-old knew how to open one, even though they might not know how to use it.

The balisong disappeared in the '50s because of the unsavory reputation attached to the switchblade, flick knives and motorcycle gangs of the period. Remember Marlon Brando in "The Wild One," James Dean in "Rebel Without a Cause" and "The Blackboard Jungle"? All knives were considered dangerous weapons in the hands of criminals, delinquents and motorcycle gang members, and the federal government went out of its way to find excuses to destroy the gangs. The switchblade and gravity knife became illegal to manufacture, import or carry across state lines under the "Switchblade Knife Act." In fact, during that era, even the motorcycle had a bad image. The Honda company spent millions of dollars in advertising to make the "Hog" acceptable.

The present resurrection of the balisong can be credited to Les de Asis, Daniel Inosanto, Jeff Imada, the Filipino martial arts, the action films of today, and the September 28, 1970, ruling that lifted the importation ban when the balisong was declared "not a switchblade knife."

In the '70s, Les de Asis used modern aerospace technology to produce the best butterfly knife ever. It took the knife world by storm, and de Asis' knife received the BLADE MAGAZINE Award of the Year for the best American-made new design. Today, he is the president of Pacific Cutlery Corporation, the only licensed manufacturer of the patented Bali-Song knife and the only registered owner of the name "Bali-Song."

Dan Inosanto began using the balisong in his Filipino martial arts demonstrations and in films. He created a balisong sequence for the movie "Killer Elite" in 1975, but it was completely cut out of the finished movie. Regrettably, members of the film crew stated, "That was the best action footage ever shot." The balisong eventually appeared in Jackie Chan's "The Big Brawl," where Dan was Ron Max's behind-the-scenes advisor. In 1981, Burt Reynolds chose Dan to portray the knife-wielding villain in "Sharkey's Machine." I even used the balisong to open a bottle of wine in a Cheech and Chong film. Other movies using the balisong, at time of publication, are: "Silent Rage," "Ten to Midnight," "Outsiders."

The balisong was evident in Jackie Chan's "The Big Brawl." Dan Inosanto taught actor Ron Max (right) how to use them.

Preservers of the Filipino arts include Les de Asis (left),
president of Pacific Cutlery, Master Sam Tendencia
(center), skilled in the ancient healing art of Hilot, and
Dan Inosanto (right).

11

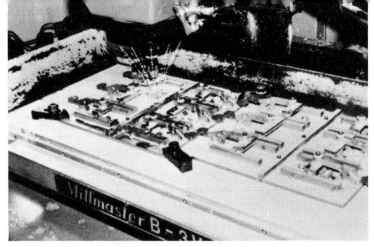

Here, space-age technology interacts with an ancient concept. This is the five-axes milling machine that produces the handles for Pacific Cutlery's balisongs with tolerances up to .0005 inch.

Knife making hasn't changed much since the 18th century. The big difference is the increased mechanization, along with the use of outside vendors of sophisticated equipment. Electric furnaces have replaced the old forges, and accurate pyrometers eliminate visual temperature determination.

All knives begin with steel, which is purchased in bars. These are "forged"—heated and then hammered until they are near the desired thickness and shape. Forging is a slow process, and the steel may have to be returned to the forge several times for reheating.

Next comes "smithing," a finer shaping technique. Smithing is followed by "tempering," which hardens the metal. Tempering is controlled by the temperature and the length of time the steel stays in the fire. It consists of heating the blade material until it is red hot (1,500-2,000 degrees Fahrenheit), then cooling the heated metal immediately by plunging it into water, oil or other substances, a process known as "quenching." Tempering is a very delicate operation. In ancient times, it was believed to be a magic step, and was often accompanied by magical incantations and secret cooling solutions. In actuality, these secret solutions assured a certain temperature but only by accident. The incantations inadvertently standardized the heating time because it took a certain amount of time to recite them.

Tempering leaves the blades very hard, but brittle. To remedy this, the blades are again heated, but at a lower temperature. When the right temperature is reached, the blades are removed and cooled slowly. The longer the blades are left in the fire, the more flexible they become.

The tempered steel is then ready for grinding, which gives the knife its finished form. In fact, a knife's efficiency and appearance is determined by the grinder. Grinding is performed by different size grinding wheels, depending on the design of the blade. Small grinding wheels are used for a small hollow ground blade, while a large flat blade needs a large diameter wheel or an abrasive belt backed by a flat platen. After grinding, the blade is sharpened and polished.

While a blade is being fashioned, the handle is simultaneously following its own course toward completion. Cutting, drilling, adding insert material, and polishing are the typical steps.

Blades and handles are finally joined and assembled along with the latches. Balisongs require many testing procedures to make sure the parts fit properly and work well. The blade must fold into the handle at the proper angle, without touching the sides, and must also lie flat, open and closed. Proper clearance, balance and play must be maintained. Before each balisong leaves the plant at Pacific Cutlery, it goes through about 85 hand and machine processes requiring roughly 24 hours of labor.

In knife jargon, the balisong is classified as a nontypical folder, a typical folder being a regular pocket-type folding knife. The balisong itself, though ancient in concept, is truly ingenious in terms of form following function. It completely eliminates the need for a blade protecting sheath. Instead, the balisong conveniently and safely stores in half its length, and the handles do double duty by sheathing the blade as well as quickly pivoting around to form a sturdy handle. The balisong is an improvement over the typical folding knife because it can be opened with one hand. The integral quillon even doubles as a thumb and finger guard by providing a protruding hilt that prevents the hand from sliding onto the blade.

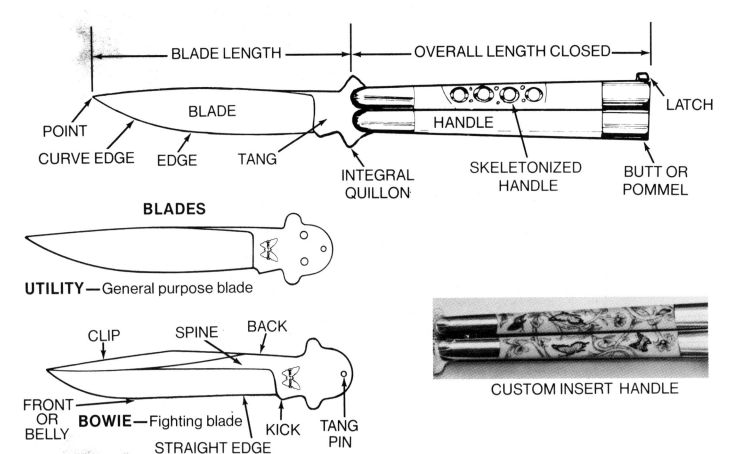

BLADE LENGTH — OVERALL LENGTH CLOSED

POINT
CURVE EDGE
BLADE
EDGE
TANG
INTEGRAL QUILLON
HANDLE
SKELETONIZED HANDLE
LATCH
BUTT OR POMMEL

BLADES

UTILITY—General purpose blade

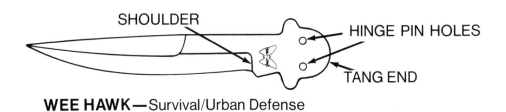

CLIP
SPINE
BACK
FRONT OR BELLY
KICK
TANG PIN
STRAIGHT EDGE

BOWIE—Fighting blade

DROP POINT—Skinning and Field Dressing

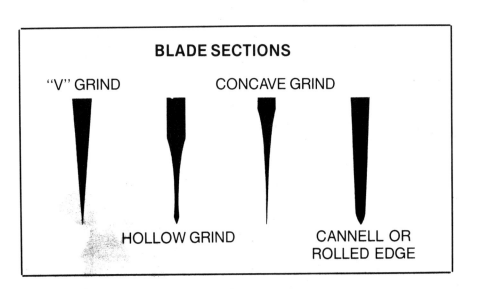

SHOULDER
HINGE PIN HOLES
TANG END

WEE HAWK—Survival/Urban Defense

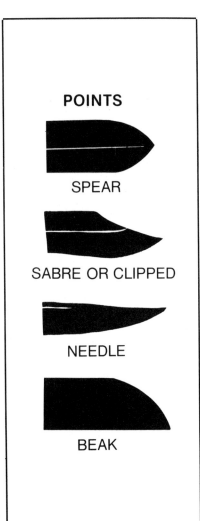

POINTS

SPEAR

SABRE OR CLIPPED

NEEDLE

BEAK

CUSTOM INSERT HANDLE

BLADE SECTIONS

"V" GRIND   CONCAVE GRIND

HOLLOW GRIND   CANNELL OR ROLLED EDGE

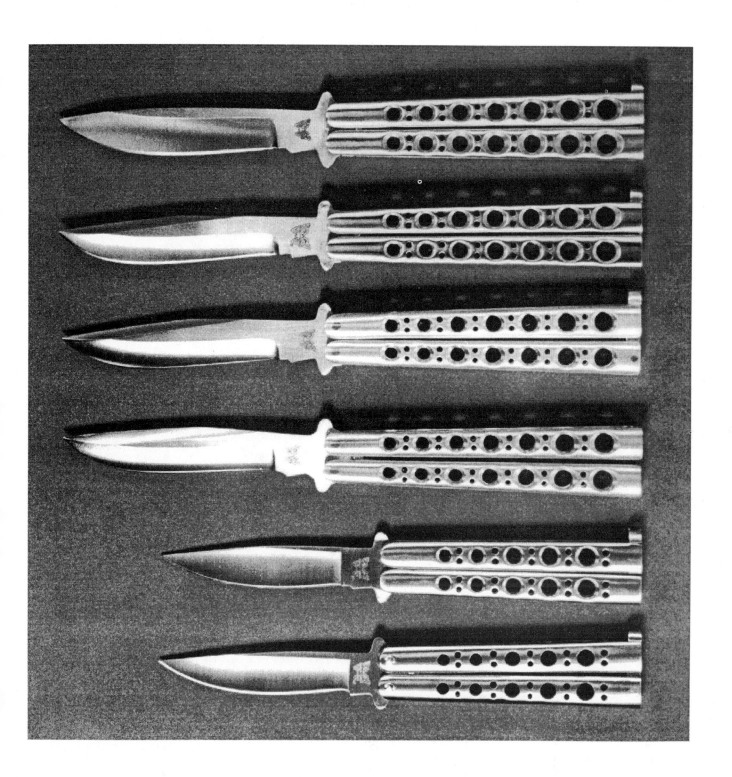

For many years, carbon steel was used for knife blades because it was easy to sharpen. But carbon steel tended to rust and stain easily. Next came the stainless-steel blade, which retained its good looks, but was harder to sharpen and to keep sharp. Today, most knife blades are made of a high-carbon stainless steel that combines the sharpness of carbon steel with the easy-care features of stainless.

Today's most common blade material is 440-C. Its first use is credited to R.W. Loveless, the founder of the Knifemakers Guild. It is also sometimes referred to as surgical steel, although surgical steel may not be as precisely blended. True 440-C contains 80.4% iron, 17.05% chromium, .5% manganese, .45% molybdenum, .4% silicon and .2% nickel.

The scale that measures the hardness of steel is known as the Rockwell C scale. The higher the number on the Rockwell scale, the harder the steel. A typical knife blade is hardened to a Rockwell C scale 58-60. This range yields a blade with good edge-holding characteristics that is not too brittle. A hardness rating in excess of 60 on the Rockwell scale may be too brittle for most general knife uses. Hard steels hold their edge longer in use, but are more difficult to sharpen. Softer blades are easier to sharpen, but lose their cutting edge more quickly.

Knife blades come in many different cross-sections and configurations, so blade choice is strictly a personal decision. I recommend that your first balisong blade have a full flat back or spine. This allows you to manipulate to your heart's content with relative safety, providing you tape up the single cutting edge first.

Once familiar and fairly proficient with the workings of a balisong, you can graduate to the modified stiletto or wee hawk blade with half (or part of the upper edge) sharp. This type of blade is preferred by survivalists and urban-defense knife fighters, because of the dual-cutting surfaces. Be careful when buying a balisong with both edges completely sharpened because, to manipulate it safely, you must be very proficient.

The best knife handles are determined by how well they fit your hands. The better the handle fits, the easier it is to use and to manipulate. Insert material is an esthetic decision, although collectors feel that ivory inserts retain their value best. Lightweight "skeletonized" handles are the most popular today. Les de Asis was the first to pioneer lightweight handles on the balisong knife. Not only are they lighter, but they also offer a better grip, much like a tread pattern on a rain tire. To maintain a lightweight handle's appearance, simply run it over a buffer to remove any scratches or nicks. Solid one-piece or insertless handles are also more practical for self-defense purposes, since you don't have to worry about the inserts popping out or cracking.

Balisong knives range in price from $2.50 to over $300. If you are looking for name brand quality, the top of the line balisongs are made by Les de Asis of Pacific Cutlery Corporation in Los Angeles, California. This top-quality knife offers prestige, the finest materials, custom craftsmanship, a ten-year guarantee, and maintenance service. Every balisong or knife lover should once in his or her life own at least one Bali-Song® especially since they hold their value and often appreciate.

Even if you can't afford the top of the line Bali-Song®, you can practice and learn with some of the mass-produced models. Here are some hints on buying balisongs. Always buy your knife from a reputable source, one that isn't known for selling "fly-by-night" junk. Buy your knives one at a time, so as not to get stuck with a bunch of junk. At worse, balisongs make great letter openers. Let me warn you, though, once you buy your first balisong, you are hooked for life and will become an avid collector. Welcome to the world of the balisong.

CARE AND TREATMENT

Just as your car and body require regular care and maintenance, so does your balisong knife. Reasonable care will assure you of a lifetime of continued fine performance.

1. KEEP THE BLADE CLEAN AND DRY AFTER USE. Even though modern knife steel is rust-resistant, it contains a very high amount of carbon to maintain its outstanding edge-holding qualities. Periodically, wipe your blade with a lightly oiled cloth to keep it in peak condition.

2. NEVER USE YOUR KNIFE AS A CHISEL, SCREWDRIVER OR PRYBAR. Prying can snap the blade or pop the rivets or pivot pins.

3. NEVER THROW A BALISONG KNIFE. It was not designed as a throwing knife and is not suited to that purpose. The impact will throw the parts out of alignment, or possibly cause the rivets to open so that the knife may come apart.

4. FOLDING KNIVES NEED LUBRICATION. An occasional drop or two of oil on the pivot points will promote smooth operation and ensure a long service life.

5. KEEP YOUR KNIFE SHARP. Sharp knives are safer than dull knives, because they cut with less pressure and so are less likely to slip. Also, the extra pressure when using a dull blade isn't good for the pivot pins in the handle assembly.

6. TREAT YOUR BALISONG WITH RESPECT. Handle it as the fine tool that it is, and a balisong will continue to serve your needs for many years.

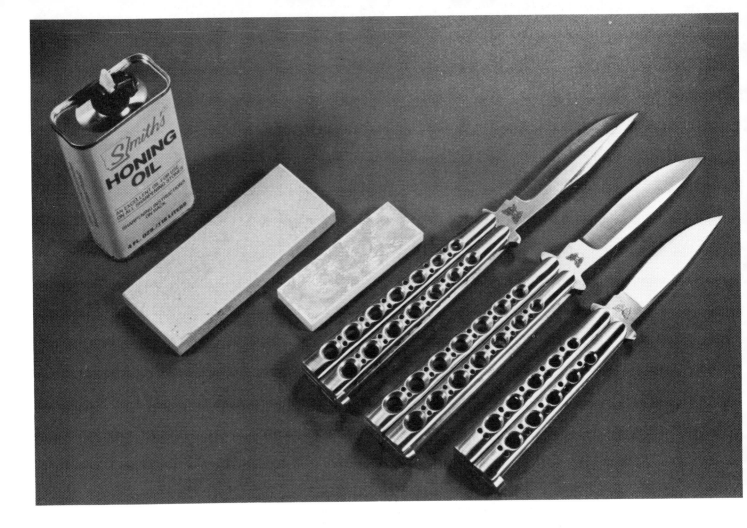

SHARPENING YOUR BALISONG

Buy a soft (medium) or hard (fine) whetstone, never a coarse stone. A small, 3-inch or 4-inch whetstone is convenient to take with you when fishing or camping, and is good to use on small knives. A larger, 5 inches or longer stone is much easier to sharpen on, however.

The most critical part of sharpening is determining the correct angle at which to hold the blade. Place the edge of the blade flat on the stone, then tilt the back edge of the blade up until you feel the bevel of the blade flatten on the stone. Too high and you dull the edge. Too shallow and you never touch the edge and work only on the bevel. Try to achieve a 20-degree angle.

The most accurate way to arrive at this angle was stated in Tom Wei Ding's book on the balisong (Sunrider Corp., N.Y.). He states, "Have a light directly overhead of the knife and sharpening stone and when it casts a shadow over the blade, make sure the shadow is even with the top of the upper part of the blade. This is the closest one can get to a perfect 20-degree angle on a flat stone."

Now that you've experimented with that elusive 20-degree angle, you are ready to start sharpening.

First clean the stone with a rag or paper towel. Coat the surface of the stone with a generous amount of honing oil (or any light oil). Never use a stone dry, because metal shavings will clog its surface and damage the stone *and* your blade.

Place the blade on the stone with the cutting edge of the blade facing away from you. Get that 20-degree angle. *Push* the knife away from you like you are trying to slice a very thin section off the top of the stone. Repeat this stroke two or three times starting from the base and working to the tip.

Now, turn the knife over to the other side of the blade, with the cutting edge facing you. Find that 20-degree angle again. *Pull* the knife toward you two or three times starting from the base and working to the tip. Following these steps puts a sharp edge on your blade.

Try to take the same number of strokes on each side of the blade. Remember to clean the stone after each use by wiping away the honing oil with a rag or paper towel.

RIGHT

WRONG

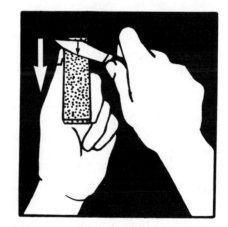

THE BALISONG AND THE LAW

First of all and most importantly, *always use good common sense.* Use good common sense with the care and handling of this knife, just as you would any other type of knife. Don't flaunt it in front of a layman, lawman or nonmartial artist, because it will appear menacing and dangerous and will probably get you in a whole lot of trouble.

Laws regarding weapons vary from state to state, and from city to city. Because of the severe penalties for carrying a weapon, always first consult your local police department.

In California, for example, the state Dangerous Weapons Control Law outlaws the possession, sale, importation or manufacture of a long list of weapons, including blackjacks, billies, nunchakus, sandclubs, brass knuckles and throwing stars. The balisong knife is not on that list. An inquiry to the local Los Angeles Police Department in regard to carrying knives was answered this way: double-edged knives or daggers are illegal; blades over 6 inches in length are illegal (4 inches in New York); and any attempt to conceal a weapon is illegal. The approved method of carrying a knife is in a case strapped onto your belt. There are specific exceptions which you can research on your own.

At one point there was a law (T.D. 71-133) that prohibited the importation of the balisong knife by classifying it as a switchblade. In the case of *United States vs. 1,044 Balisong Knives,* Civil No. 70-110, September 28, 1970, the court held the balisong knife not to be a switchblade within the meaning of 16 U.S.C. 1241. It was found that all balisong-design knives should be subjected to the same scrutiny as are all other pocket knives to ensure their admissibility under the Switchblade Knife Act. T.D. 71-133 was overruled. If you are innocently questioned about the knife by someone unfamiliar to you or by the authorities, remember to tell them it is just a pocket knife and show them how to open it—slowly with *both* hands.

Here are excerpts from the California Penal Code Book pertaining to knives and the law:

§ **626.10** (a) Any person, except a duly appointed peace officer, a full-time paid peace officer of another state of the federal government who is carrying out official duties while in this state, any person summoned by any such officer to assist in making arrests or preserving the peace while he is actually engaged in assisting any such officer, or a member of the military forces of this state or the United States who is engaged in the performance of his duties, who brings or possesses any dirk, dagger, knife having a blade longer than 3½ inches, folding knife with a blade that locks into place, or razor with an unguarded blade upon the grounds of, or within, any public school providing instruction in kindergarten or any of grades 1 through 12, inclusive, is guilty of a misdemeanor.

(b) Any person, except a duly appointed peace officer, a full-time paid peace officer of another state or the federal government who is carrying out official duties while in this state, any person summoned by any such officer to assist in making arrests or preserving the peace while he is actually engaged in assisting any such officer, or a member of the military forces of this state or the United States who is engaged in the performance of his duties, who brings or possesses any dirk, dagger, or knife having a fixed blade longer than 3½ inches upon the grounds of, or within, any state university, state college, or community college, is guilty of a misdemeanor.

(c) Subdivisions (a) and (b) shall not apply to any person who brings or possesses a knife having a blade longer than 3½ inches or razor with an unguarded blade upon the grounds of, or within, a public school providing instruction in kindergarten or any of grades 1 through 12, inclusive, or any state university, state college, or community college, at the direction of a certificated or classified employee of the school for use in a school sponsored activity or class.

(d) Subdivisions (a) and (b) shall not apply to any person who brings or possesses a knife having a blade longer than 3½ inches or razor with an unguarded blade upon the grounds of, or within, a public school providing instruction in kindergarten or any of grades 1 through 12, inclusive, or any state university, state college, or community college, for a lawful purpose within the scope of his employment.

(e) Subdivision (b) shall not apply to any person who brings or possesses a knife having a fixed blade longer than 3½ inches upon the grounds of, or within, any state university, state college, or community college, for lawful use in or around a residence or residential facility located upon such grounds or for lawful use in food preparation or consumption, within the scope of his employment.

(f) Any certificated or classified employee of a public school providing instruction in kindergarten or any of grades 1 through 12, inclusive, may seize any of the weapons described in subdivision (a), and any certificated or classified employee of any state university, state college, or community college may seize any of the weapons described in subdivision (b) from the possession of any person upon the grounds of, or within, the school if he knows or has reasonable cause to know the person is prohibited from bringing or possessing the weapon upon the grounds of, or within, the school.

§ **653k.** Every person who carries upon his person, and every person who sells, offers for sale, exposes for sale, loans, transfers, or gives to any other person a switch-blade knife having a blade over two inches in length is guilty of a misdemeanor.

For the purposes of this section a "switch-blade knife" is a knife having the appearance of a pocket-knife, and shall include a spring-blade knife, snap-blade knife, gravity knife or any other similar type knife; the blade or blades of which are two or more inches long and which can be released automatically by a flick of a button, pressure on the handle, flip of the wrist or other mechanical device, or is released by the weight of the blade or by any type of mechanism whatsoever.

§ **12002.** (a) Nothing in this chapter prohibits police officers, special police officers, peace officers, or law enforcement officers from carrying any wooden club, baton, or any equipment authorized for the enforcement of law or ordinance in any city or county.

(b) Nothing in this chapter prohibits a uniformed security guard, regularly employed and compensated as such by a person engaged in any lawful business, while actually employed and engaged in protecting and preserving property or life within the scope of his or her employment, from carrying any wooden club or baton if the uniformed security guard has satisfactorily completed a course of instruction certified by the Department of Consumer Affairs in the carrying and use of the club or baton. The training institution certified by the Department of Consumer Affairs to present this course, whether public or private, is authorized to charge a fee covering the cost of the training.

(c) The Department of Consumer Affairs, in cooperation with the Commission on Peace Officer Standards and Training, shall develop standards for a course in the carrying and use of the club or baton.

(d) Any uniformed security guard who successfully completes a course of instruction under this section is entitled to receive a permit to carry and use a club or baton within the scope of his or her employment, issued by the Department of Consumer Affairs. The department may authorize certified training institutions to issue permits to carry and use a club or baton. A fee in the amount provided by law shall be charged by the Department of Consumer Affairs to offset the costs incurred by the department in course certification, quality control activities associated with the course and issuance of the permit.

(e) Any person who has received a permit or certificate which indicates satisfactory completion of a club or baton training course approved by the Commission on Peace Officer Standards and Training prior to January 1, 1983, shall not be required to obtain a baton or club permit or complete a course certified by the Department of Consumer Affairs.

§ **12020.** (a) Any person in this state who manufactures or causes to be manufactured, imports into the state, keeps for sale, or offers or exposes for sale, or who gives, lends, or possesses any cane gun or wallet gun, any firearm which is not immediately recognizable as a firearm, any ammunition which contains or consists of any flechette dart, any bullet containing or carrying an explosive agent, or any instrument or weapon of the kind commonly known as a blackjack, slungshot, billy, nunchaku, sandclub, sandbag, sawed-off shotgun, or metal knuckles, or who carries concealed upon his person any explosive substance, other than fixed ammunition or who carries concealed upon his person any dirk or dagger, is guilty of a felony, and upon conviction shall be punishable by imprisonment in the county jail not exceeding one year or in a state prison. A bullet containing or carrying an explosive agent is not a destructive device as that term is used in Section 12301.

(b) Subdivision (a) shall not apply to any of the following:

(1) The manufacture, possession, transportation or use, with blank cartridges, of sawed-off shotguns solely as props for motion picture film or television program production when such is authorized by the Department of Justice pursuant to Article 6 (commencing with Section 12095) of this chapter and is not in violation of federal law.

(2) The possession of a nunchaku on the premises of a school which holds a regulatory or business license and teaches the arts of self-defense.

(3) The manufacture of a nunchaku for sale to, or the sale of a nunchaku to, a school which holds a regulatory or business license and teaches the arts of self-defense.

(c) Any person in this state who manufactures or causes to be manufactured, imports into the state, keeps for sale, or offers or exposes for sale, or who gives, lends, or possesses any instrument, without handles, consisting of a metal plate having three or more radiating points with one or more sharp edges and designed in the shape of a polygon, trefoil, cross, star, diamond, or other geometric shape for use as a weapon for throwing is guilty of a felony, and upon conviction shall be punishable by imprisonment in the county jail not exceeding one year or in a state prison.

(2) As used in this section, a "nunchaku" means an instrument consisting of two or more sticks, clubs, bars or rods to be used as handles, connected by a rope, cord, wire or chain, in the design of a weapon used in connection with the practice of a system of self-defense such as karate.

(3) As used in this section a "wallet gun" means any firearm mounted or enclosed in a case, resembling a wallet, designed to be or capable of being carried in a pocket or purse, if such firearm may be fired while mounted or enclosed in such case.

(4) As used in this section a "cane gun" means any firearm mounted or enclosed in a stick, staff, rod, crutch or similar device, designed to be or capable of being used as an aid in walking, if such firearm may be fired while mounted or enclosed therein.

(5) As used in this section, a "flechette dart" means a dart, capable of being fired from a firearm, which measures approximately one inch in length with tail fins which take up five-sixteenths inch of the body.

(e) Knives carried in sheaths which are worn openly suspended from the waist of the wearer are not concealed within the meaning of this section.

§ **12029.** Except as provided in Section 12020, blackjacks, slungshots, billies, nunchakus, sandclubs, sandbags, metal knuckles, any instrument described in subdivision (c) of Section 12020, and sawed-off shotguns as defined in Section 12020 are nuisances. Such weapons shall be subject to confiscation and summary destruction whenever found within the state. Such weapons shall be destroyed in Section 12028, except that upon the certification of a judge or of the district attorney that the ends of justice will be subserved thereby, such weapons shall be reserved until the necessity for its use ceases.

CARRYING THE BALISONG

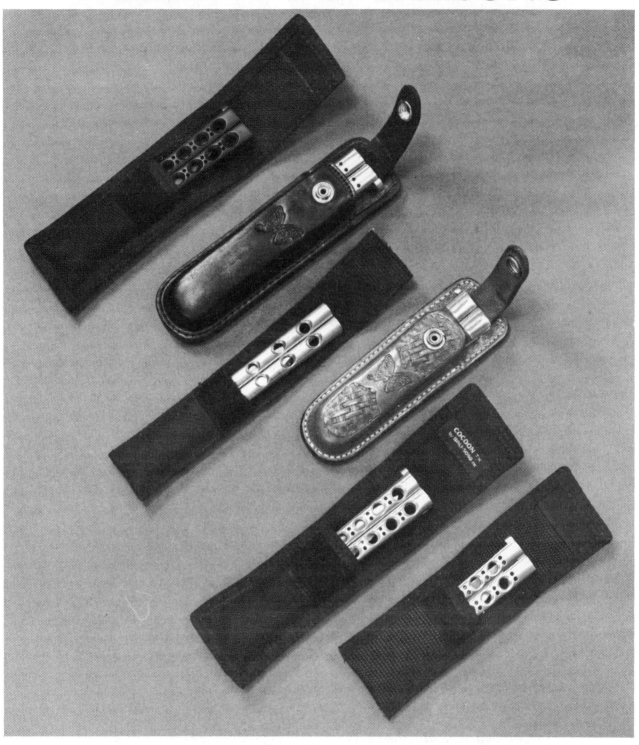

The legal or approved way to carry your balisong is in a leather case or
Cocoon™ strapped onto your belt. The horizontal or vertical Cocoons shown
are made of ballistic nylon with a Velcro closure. They are comfortable,
accessible, strong and attract little attention. Cocoons were designed and named
by Les de Asis of Pacific Cutlery, while he was driving down Highway 17 at 1:30
a.m. on his way to a knife show in San Jose, California. "Every butterfly comes
from a cocoon," was his brainstorm.

Carrying positions involve those areas on the body or clothing where a balisong can be placed or positioned for easy access. There are two types of carries: obvious (legal) carries, where the knife is exposed and visible, and the illegal carries, where the balisong is hidden from view. The concealed carries are inserted for the sake of professional soldiers, bodyguards, law-enforcement officers or anyone faced with an inescapable, life-threatening, self-defense type situation.

The key to a good carrying position is one in which the weapon can be quickly and smoothly drawn without any wasted time or motion. The specific locations are best selected according to your personal preference, dexterity or whether you are left or right-handed. It is to your advantage to know and practice with all locations, though. Dan Inosanto always stresses being prepared for any and every situation. You never know when your right hand might be neutralized or immobilized.

If you are anticipating an inescapable attack, preparatory arrangements can be made to conceal the balisong. Ed Parker, the Father of American Karate, has often said, "One who is truly prepared appears as if he is not prepared at all." To look unprepared builds false confidence in your assailant. By contrast, looking prepared, obviously armed, and knowledgeable places your opponent doubly on guard.

But more importantly, you must be totally familiar with the balisong's use, operation and your own abilities and limitations. You must be totally prepared to use the knife in an emergency self-defense situation. Any hesitation or lack of expertise will result in your attacker taking your weapon away from you, and turning it against you. If you have any doubt about your capabilities, you're probably better off leaving your knife at home.

A knife is a tool of maximum force that can seriously injure or even kill. It, therefore, must never be drawn unless absolutely necessary. In ancient times many cultures decreed that no sword or blade should be unsheathed unless your intention was to draw blood. There were, of course, "proper" ways to draw the blade for cleaning or sharpening without bloodshed. But if the blade was drawn improperly and no blood was shed combatively, the only way to return the blade to its sheath was to first cut yourself.

Today these ancient rituals are no longer practiced. The unsheathing of most blades are done without discrimination or hesitation. Drawing a straight blade is usually done in one motion, while a typical folding knife is drawn and opened with two hands. The balisong, however, can be drawn, opened and closed in one spectacular one-handed motion.

The following techniques require practice and more practice. Your draw should flow without hesitation, loss of motion, or thought, because it is from the draw that your defense is initiated. Condition yourself to always initiate your action from the draw. Formulate your own ideas, since space limitations prevent us from including them all.

HORIZONTAL DRAW (latch side up and out)

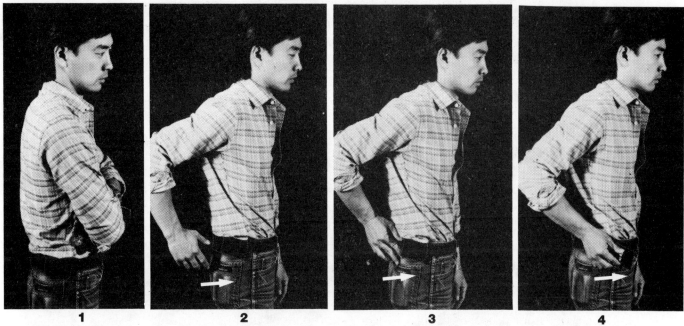

1   2   3   4

This draw calls for a smooth continuous movement. The cocoon cover is slid open and the knife is grabbed in one continuous motion.

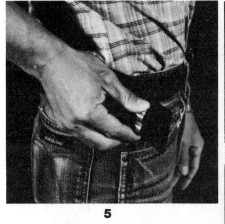

5

The placement of the knife (latch side up and out) calls for a reverse ice pick opening (see chapter on manipulation). The latch is popped open in photo 7.

6   7   8

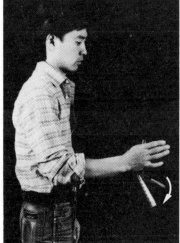

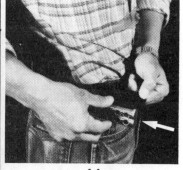

9   10   11

Always replace the knife exactly the same way to facilitate the next opening without having to think about it.

HORIZONTAL DRAW (tang side out/latch in)

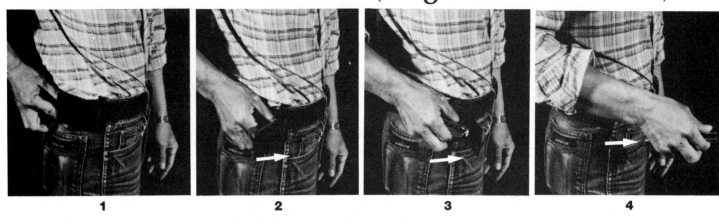

1   2   3   4

This drawing motion is similar to the previous one. The difference is that here the knife is inserted with the latch inside. The latch is automatically popped in photo (4) as soon as it clears the cocoon.

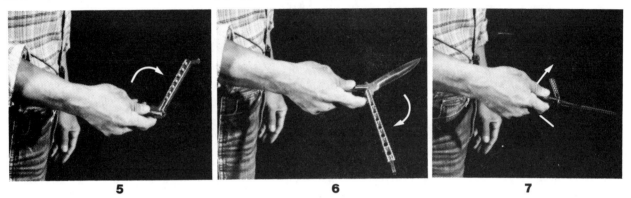

5   6   7

Flip handle up (5 and 6). Let handle twist one-half turn clockwise (7) while handle continues flowing.

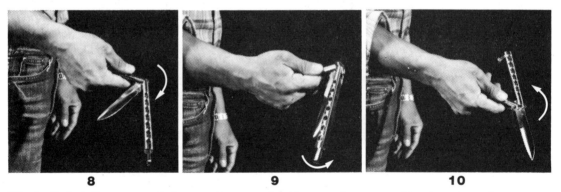

8   9   10

The knife briefly stops and changes direction (8). Reverse direction of knife and catch upcoming handle (9, 10, 11).

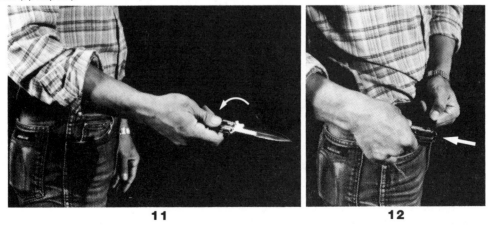

11   12

Replace knife exactly the same.

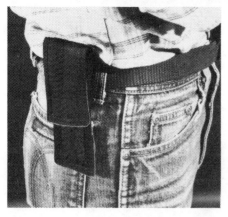

Cocoon in vertical industrial carrying position.

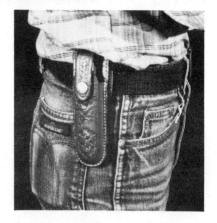

Leather case in vertical industrial carrying position.

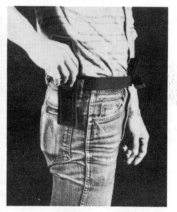

This draw is like opening a flap pocket on your clothing and withdrawing a pencil. It is more time-consuming and doesn't lend itself to instantaneous self-defense action. This is a good industrial carrying method, though.

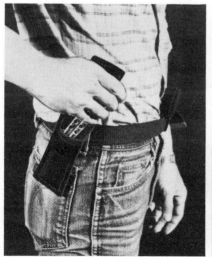
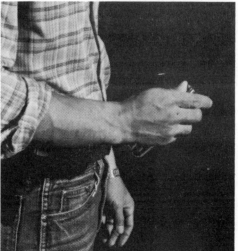

The vertical latch up position of the knife calls for an ice pick opening (see chapter on manipulation).

VERTICAL DROP CARRY

Vertical drop carry with tang side down.

Vertical drop carry with latch side down.

 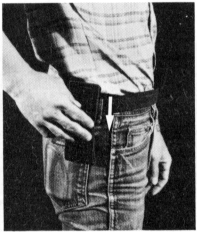  

This is a vertical drop carry. The cocoon is opened and the knife is retrieved in one fluid motion.

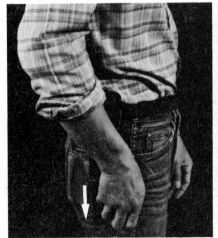 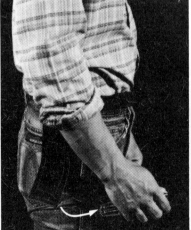 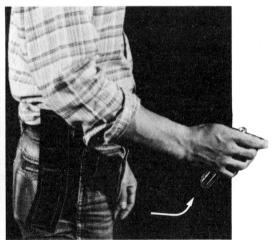

The only disadvantage to this carry is that the knife might accidentally fall out.

HORIZONTAL CROSS DRAW

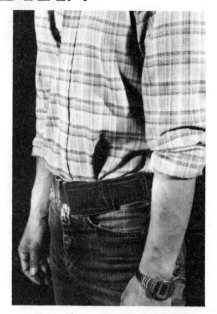

For a left-handed person, the balisong would be placed on the right hip.

This draw is effective when initiated from a casual arms-crossed position.

The disadvantage is that by reaching over to your left side, your whole right side is left vulnerable unless you safety check with your left hand.

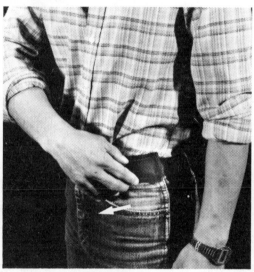
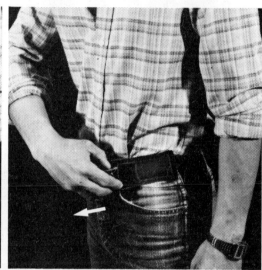

1   **2**   **3**

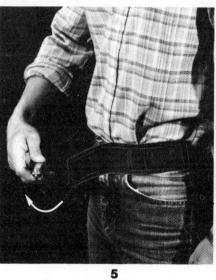

4   **5**   **6**

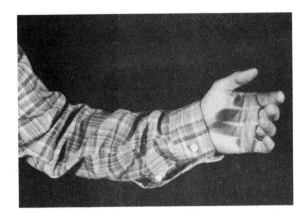

CONCEALED WRIST CARRY
(shown exposed)

This carry works best with a western-type shirt with snaps instead of buttons.

Reach into the cuff slot and rip open the Velcro cover, which will in turn pop the snap on your cuff and you can withdraw the knife in one upward motion.

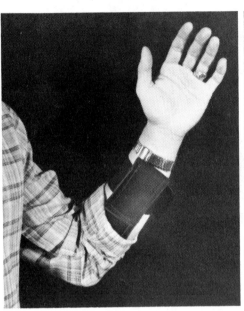

1

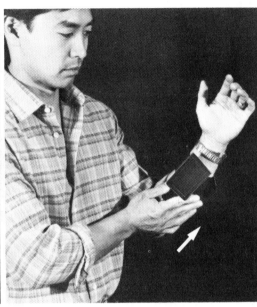

2

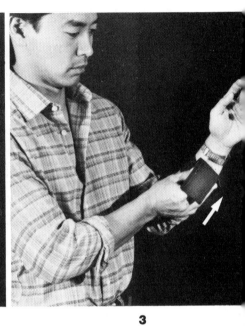

3

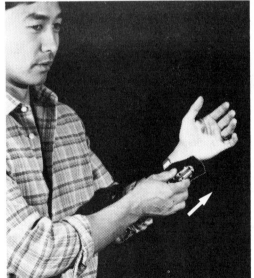

4

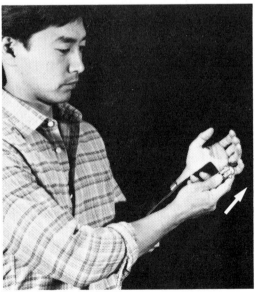

5

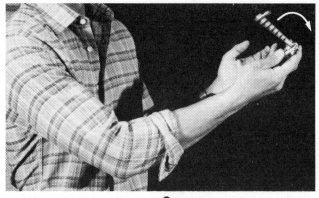

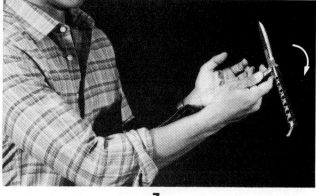

6

7

The position of the knife again dictates the opening method.

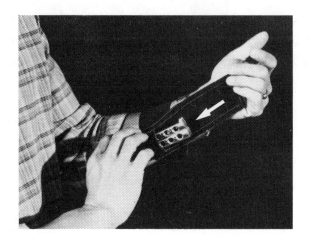

Always replace the knife to facilitate the desired opening.

CONCEALED LEG DROP AND ANKLE DRAW CARRY

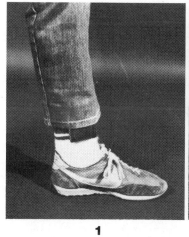

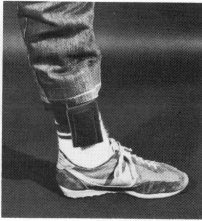

1

2

3

CONCEALED SHOULDER DRAW (shown exposed)

Carry would be under the shirt, just like a shoulder holster for a gun.

1   2   3   4

Velcro, a unique "hook and loop" fastening system for applications where repeated separation and rejoining of components is necessary, is the technology that makes many of these creative carries possible. Velcro is lightweight, has blind fastening capability and is nonmetallic, nonrusting, nonjamming, quick fastening and sure release.

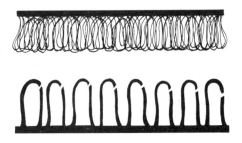

A magnified cross-section shows hundreds of minute hooks and loops on opposing sides of the material.

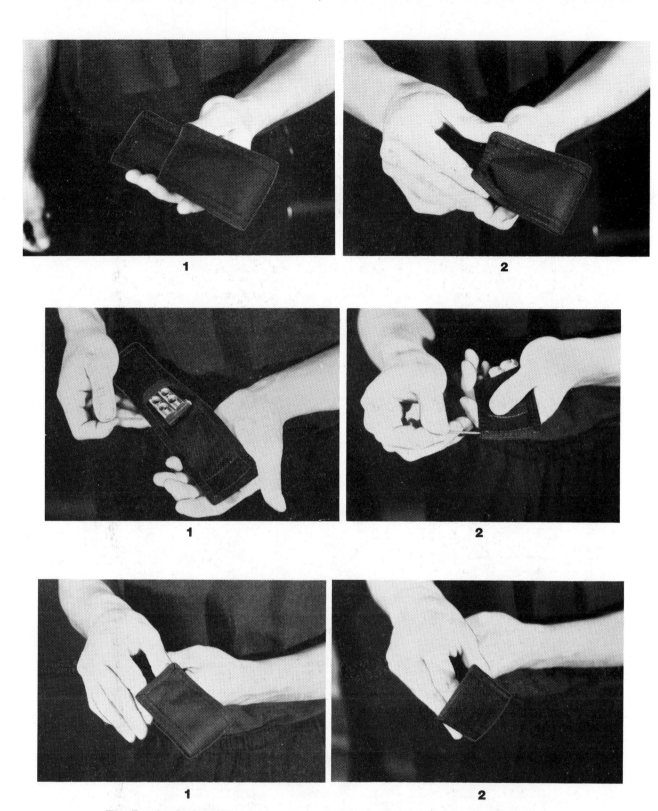

The Pacific Cutlery Cocoons work very well just as they are, but some knife fighters prefer to stiffen the opening flap by inserting a two-inch brad inside the cover flap. This allows you to open the flap and draw the knife in one smooth motion.

KNIFE SAFETY—
YOUR RESPONSIBILITY

SAFETY MUST BE THE FIRST AND CONSTANT CONSIDERATION OF EVERYONE WHO HANDLES A BALISONG.

It is your legal and moral obligation to handle, carry and use your balisong in such a manner as to prevent any accident from occurring.

Before you attempt to use a balisong in any way, READ THIS COMPLETE MANUAL CAREFULLY. With the manual in hand, practice all the steps relating to the operation of the balisong. Practice repeatedly, until you can go through each step with absolute confidence. Your goal should be to familiarize yourself with the weapon until it is like a natural extension of your hands.

The author and publisher assume no liabilities whatsoever for any injury which may occur by using the manual or by using or manipulating the Filipino balisong knife.

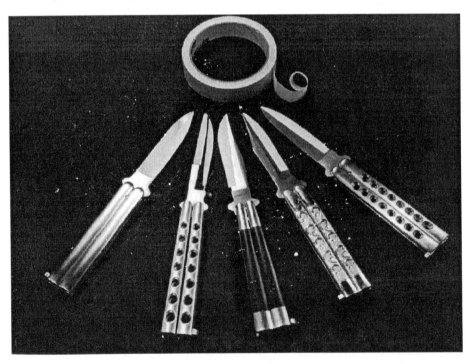

WARNING: TAPE ALL THE SHARP EDGES OF YOUR BLADE NOW!
I guarantee you will get cut if you don't. Don't remove the tape until you have finished reading and have tried the exercises two or three times.

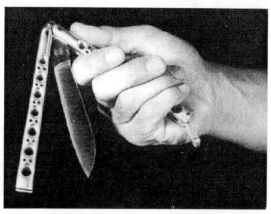

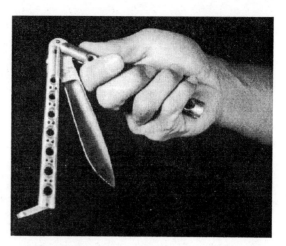

The WRONG way to hold the balisong. Note the cutting edge of the blade hitting your fingers. You WILL get cut.

The RIGHT way to hold the balisong. Note the back side of the blade hitting your fingers. You WON'T get cut.

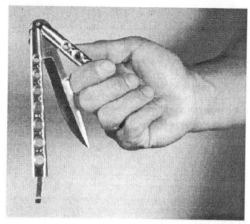

Always hold the handle with the back of the blade (flat, unsharp edge) hitting your fingers.

If your balisong has 1½ sharp edges (shown) choke up on the handle to avoid getting cut. You will learn, also, to pull back on the blade at just the right moment to prevent the blade from touching your hand at all.

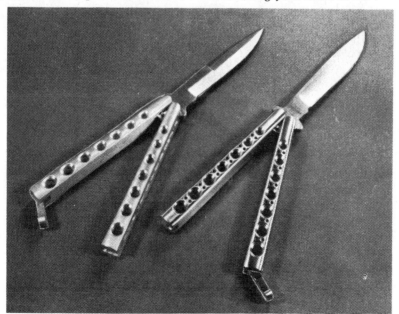

Don't use the latch to determine which handle to hold. On some models, the latch is on the opposite handle. ALWAYS hold the handle with the back (noncutting) side of the blade hitting your fingers.

COMMON CUTS

These are some of the common cuts you will get during manipulation if you don't tape up the blade until you are familiar and proficient with the balisong knife.

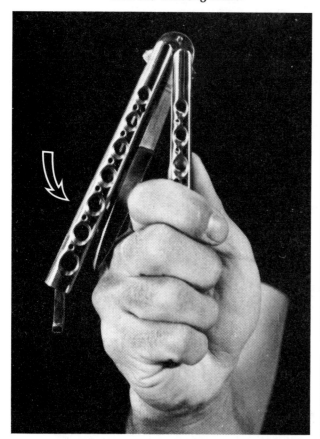

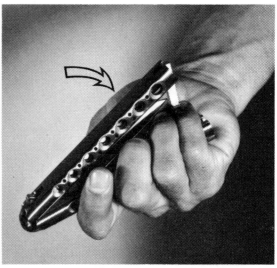

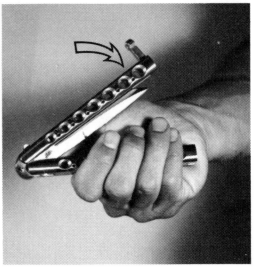

COMMON CUTS
continued

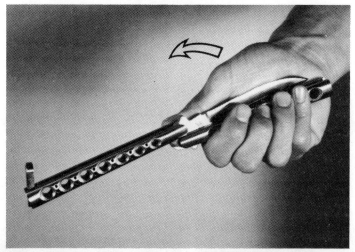

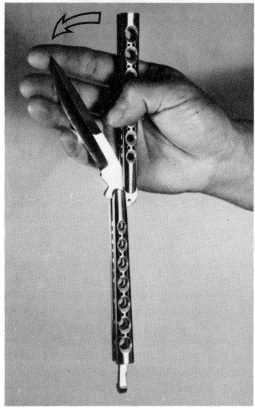

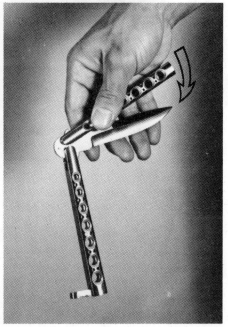

FIRST AID

In case of severe bleeding, it is essential first to stop the bleeding, then to get medical assistance. Bleeding from cuts can usually be controlled by applying direct pressure to the wound.

1. Make a pad of clean cloth, using a handkerchief or clothing.
2. Place pad on wound.
3. If the wound is on an extremity, elevate that extremity above the victim's head if possible.
4. Press and hold pad until bleeding stops. Most bleeding will stop within 5 to 15 minutes.

THE GRIP

To master the balisong, the practitioner should develop as strong a grip as possible without being unduly rigid. Keeping all fingers too tight restricts the mobility of the wrist, and unnecessarily taxes the forearm. Here is a random selection of grips to help you better understand the weapon.

The "ice pick" grip gets its name from picking ice, and for that chore it is perfect. It provides great force, but offers limited flexibility. It was used by the knights in the Middle Ages to pierce through armor, and is also a favorite in movies like "Psycho" that call for dramatic stabbing scenes.

Ice pick with cutting edge in offers a very limited cutting surface.

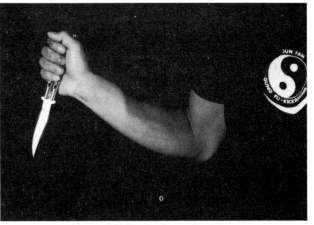

Ice pick with cutting edge out provides more cutting surface.

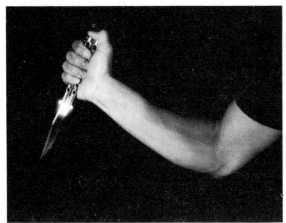

Modified ice pick with cutting edge in. The wider hand span provides more strength and wrist stability.

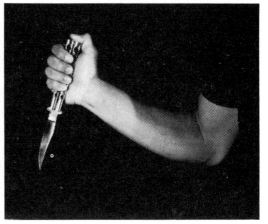

Modified ice pick with cutting edge out.

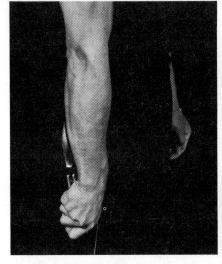
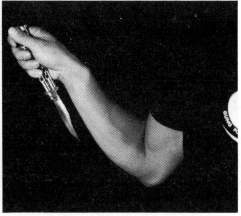

The ice pick grip with cutting edge out can become a very effective fighting tool by merely bringing the blade parallel to your arm. It is a favorite street fighter's grip. Notice the knife is practically invisible and can do great harm to an unsuspecting attacker.

The "hatchet" grip resembles a man holding a hatchet. It is good for a strong underhand stab, since the thumb is protected from a heavy impact. It is also good for a butt strike. As shown, it offers good vertical mobility.

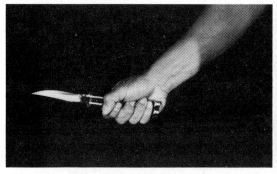
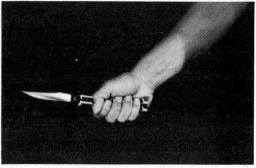

Reverse hatchet grip with cutting edge up.

Hatchet grip with cutting edge down.

The "sabre" grip offers great total mobility with the thumb guiding the blade and giving support. This grip is not good for hard stabs without a high quillon to prevent the thumb from sliding onto the blade.

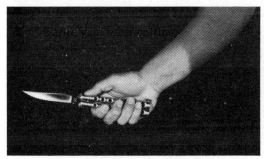
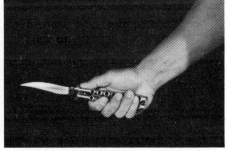

Sabre grip with cutting edge down.

Reverse sabre grip with cutting edge up.

Sabre grip for the chambered balisong limits the striking area to the knife tang.

The "foil" grip is taken from the grip used on the French fencing foil. As shown with the balisong, it offers good lateral mobility.

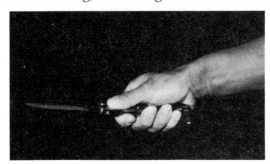

Foil grip.

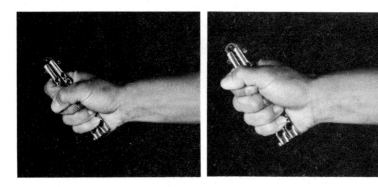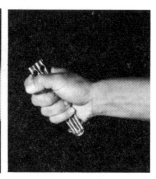

Various yawara style grips for the chambered balisong. Vary the thumb position for personal preference, strength and mobility. Note that you can strike with the front and back parts of the weapon.

STRIKING AREAS OF THE BALISONG

The balisong is a very versatile weapon. It can be used for parrying, thrusting, striking, slashing, poking, hooking, choking, locking, pinching and flailing.

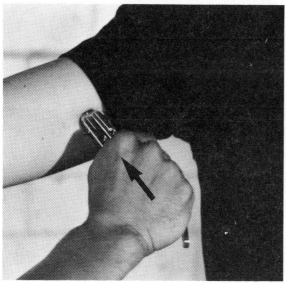

Tang jab

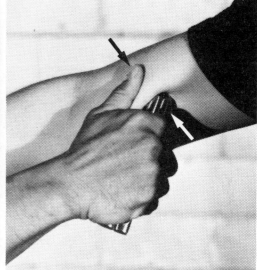

Tang pinch

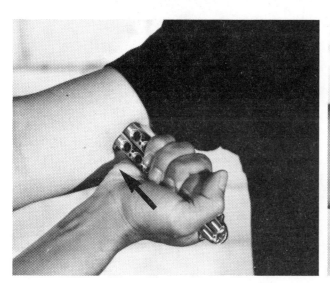

Butt strike

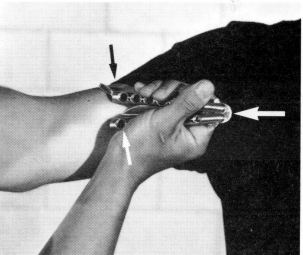

Butt stab and pinch

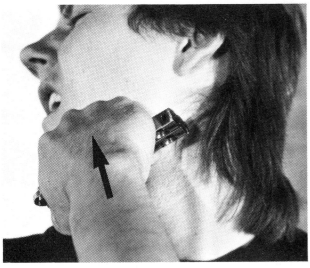

Hand-load

Handle flail

Joint strike

Wrist lock

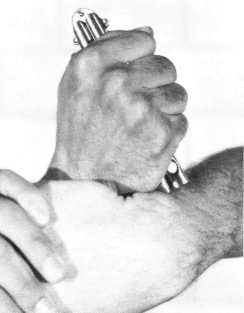

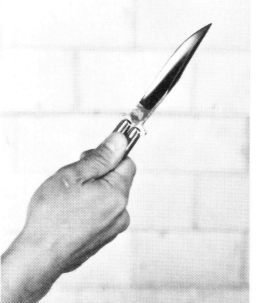

Bent arm lock

Full combat or killing mode

MANIPULATING THE BALISONG

The grip plays an integral part in assuring continuous action with the balisong. Without it you can lose the weapon or restrict its action. Remember to alternately relax and then tighten the grip on the handle as you rotate the knife or initiate the action. Try to relax your wrist while retaining control of the knife with your fingers. When the wrist is free, speed is enhanced, and maneuverability is assured.

With constant practice you develop a feel for every movement. In time, practice will enable you to control the balisong almost unconsciously. Moreover, practicing with the balisong is a lot of fun and you won't be able to put it down. As a matter of fact, balisongs have been called the "macho pacifier," since so many burly martial artists are constantly playing with them for relaxation and dexterity enhancement. The balisong is also a flashy device to impress your friends and to discourage your enemies.

The easiest way to master the examples shown in this book are to break them down into small groups and master one segment at a time. For instance, if there is a routine with 18 moves, simply isolate the groups by practicing steps 1-4, 5-8, 9-12, and 13-18 separately. After mastering the individual groups, you can finally join them all together and have the whole routine down pat. It is easier and faster to learn in this manner.

Before you start each technique, be sure to determine where the back side of the blade is located in relation to the example pictured and in relation to your own knife. Make sure you are holding the correct handle (don't go by the latch location alone).

LATCH POP AND HANDLE ADJUSTMENT TECHNIQUE

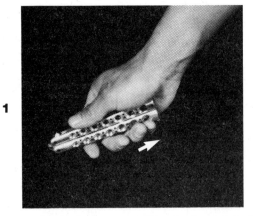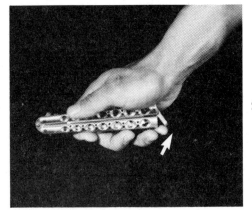

Pop latch with little finger (1 and 2).

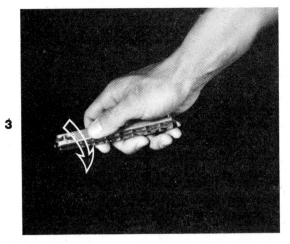

Rotate handle one-half turn counter-clockwise (3).

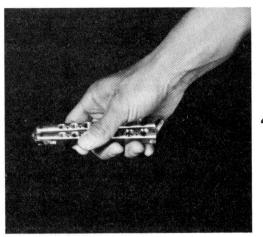

Grab latchless or "safe" handle (4).

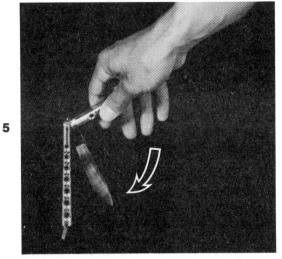

Drop or swing opposing handle. Note that the cutting edge is pointing away from the fingers.

SINGLE FLIP UP OPENING AND CLOSING

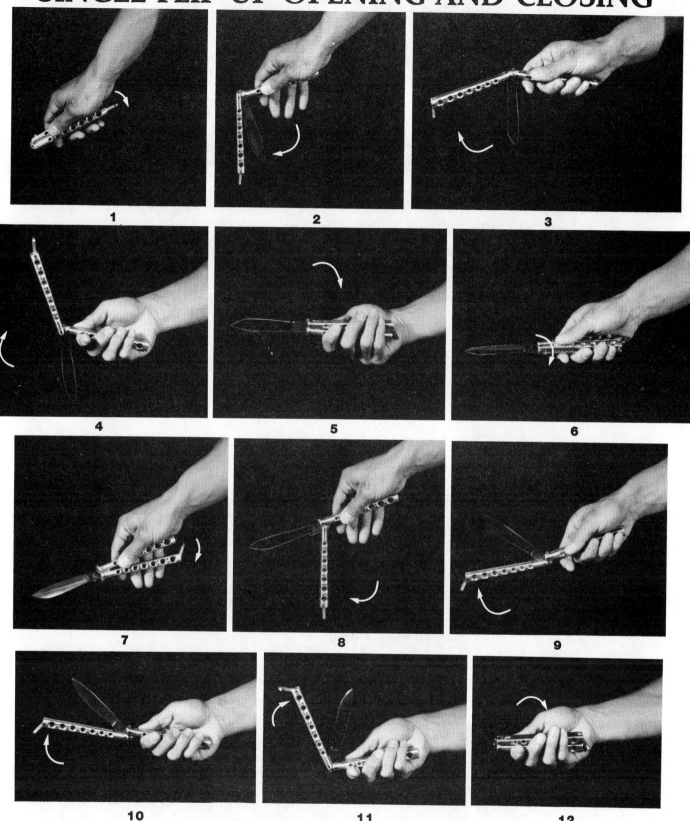

1

2

3

4

5

6

7

8

9

10

11

12

The "safe" handle is already in position so no handle adjustment is necessary (1). Drop and swing lower handle up (2 and 3). As soon as lower handle is dropped, prepare to accept the upcoming handle by turning your palm up (4). Palm up position catches upcoming handle (5). From fighting position, rotate knife and palm a half turn counterclockwise to prepare for closing (6). Release lower handle (7). Swing handle and blade up (8). Make hand adjustment to accept upcoming blade and handle (9, 10, 11 and 12). Practice these moves continuously in sets of 12 with both hands. Feel free to make slight adjustments to facilitate the moves.

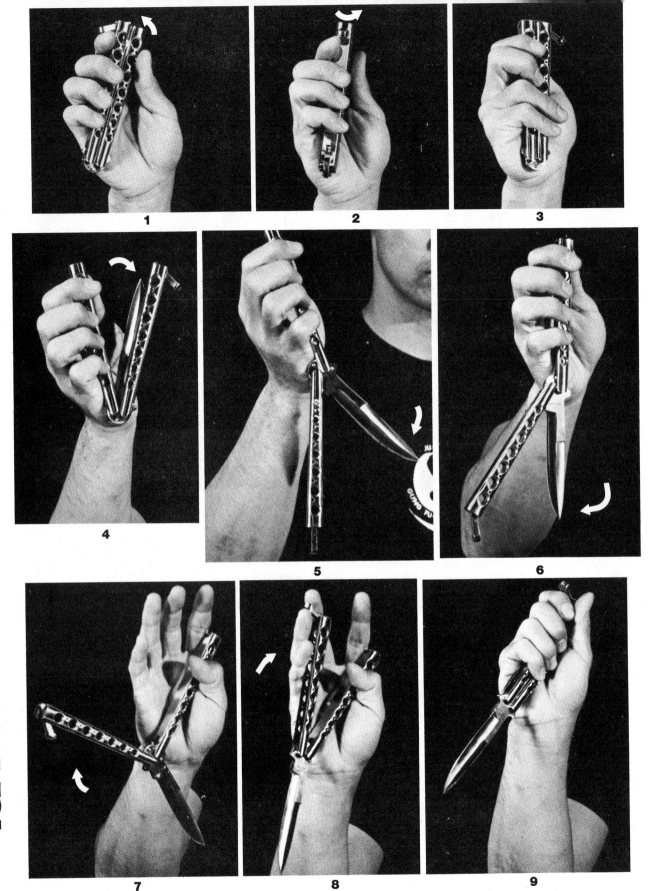

Pop latch with thumb (1). Rotate handle a half turn to grip "safe" handle (2 and 3). With fingers only gripping the "safe" handle, release and swing the opposing handle down and out (4). Adjust hand to accept upcoming handle by changing grip on "safe" handle. Use thumb and palm to hold "safe" handle, while opening fingers to accept upswing handle (5, 6 and 7). Close fingers and hand. Your knife should end up in an ice pick grip (8 and 9).

FORWARD DROP AND CATCH OPENING
(edge in)

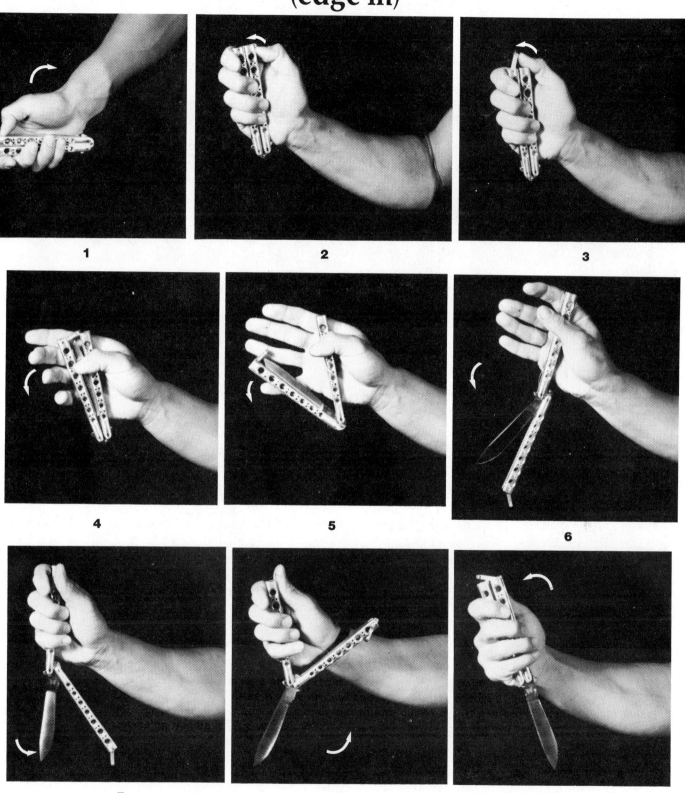

Pop latch with thumb (1, 2 and 3). Hold "safe" handle with palm and thumb (4). Drop and swing opposing handle around and up (5). Change from a thumb and palm grip to a fingers grip and move your thumb out of the way to accept the upcoming handle (6, 7, 8 and 9).

FORWARD DROP AND CATCH CLOSING
(edge in)

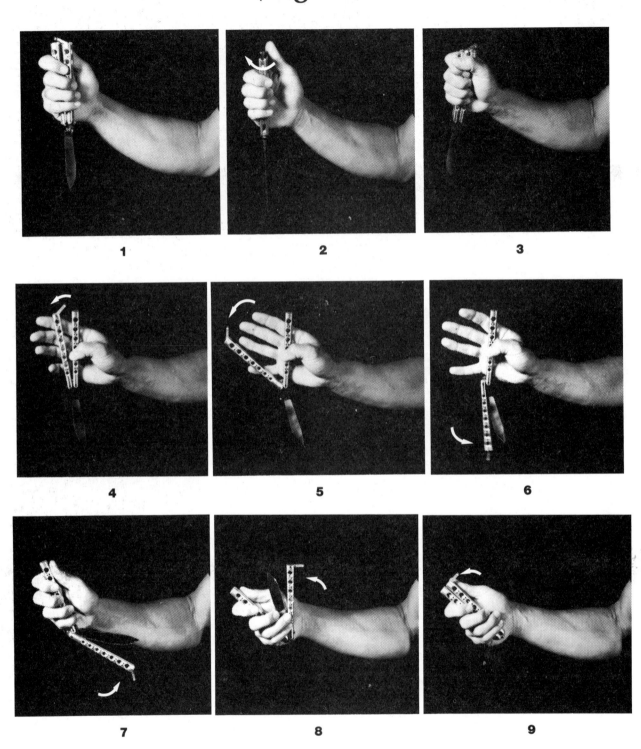

1

2

3

4

5

6

7

8

9

Rotate open knife a half turn to grip "safe" handle with thumb and palm (1, 2, 3 and 4). Drop and swing opposing handle around and up (5). Change thumb and palm grip to an all fingers grip and prepare to catch the upcoming blade and handle (6, 7, 8 and 9). Practice the previous opening and this closing together continuously 12 times and you will understand the necessary hand adjustments.

FORWARD DROP AND CATCH CLOSING (edge out)

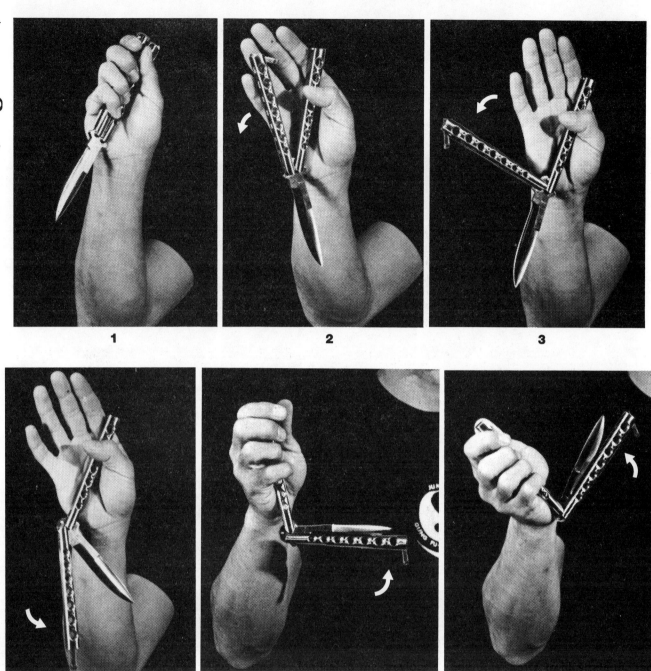

1

2

3

4

5

6

7

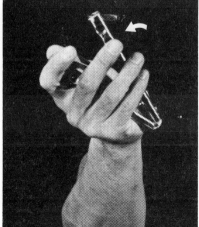

This closing is identical to the previous closing. It is shown to illustrate the fact that the handle does not always have to be rotated a half turn, since the safe handle is already in the correct position for manipulation. Write in your own hints for this closing under the photos.

1

2

3

4

5

6

7

8

9

10

11

12

13

Be sure to tape your blade before practicing this maneuver. Pop latch with thumb (1 and 2). Grab latch and let handle drop (3). Flick wrist up to provide momentum for latchless handle to swing upward (4, 5 and 6). Prepare fingers to accept upcoming handle (7 and 8). Close fingers around completed opening (9). Retain latch and prepare to drop handle for closing (10 and 11). Use fingers and wrist to give added momentum for continuation of upward movement. As blade continues up, move your thumb out of the way to prepare for the catch (12 and 13).

THUMB AND INDEX FINGER
SIDE FLIP

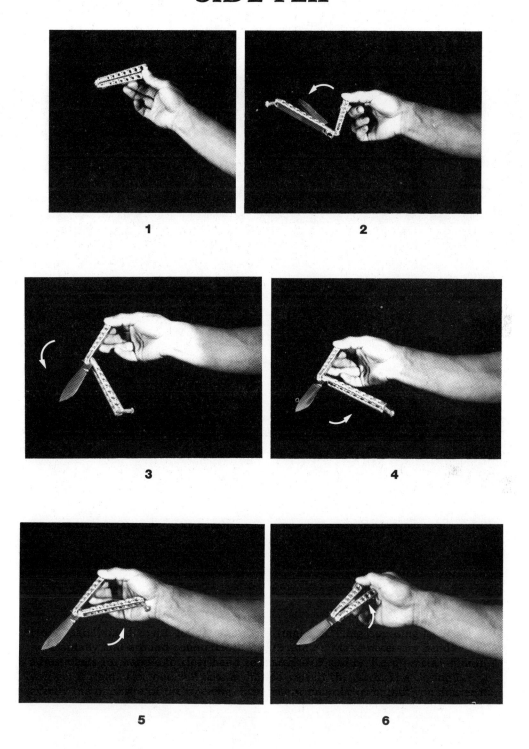

1

2

3

4

5

6

Hold "safe" handle with thumb and index finger (1). Fling opposing handle horizontally and around counterclockwise (2 and 3). Make necessary hand adjustments for handle to clear hand for catch (4, 5 and 6). Keep practicing until you get it right. This one will take awhile to perfect the catch. The closing is exactly the opposite of the opening. Experiment on your own until you master it. Practice them together.

HORIZONTAL DOUBLE FLIP OPENING

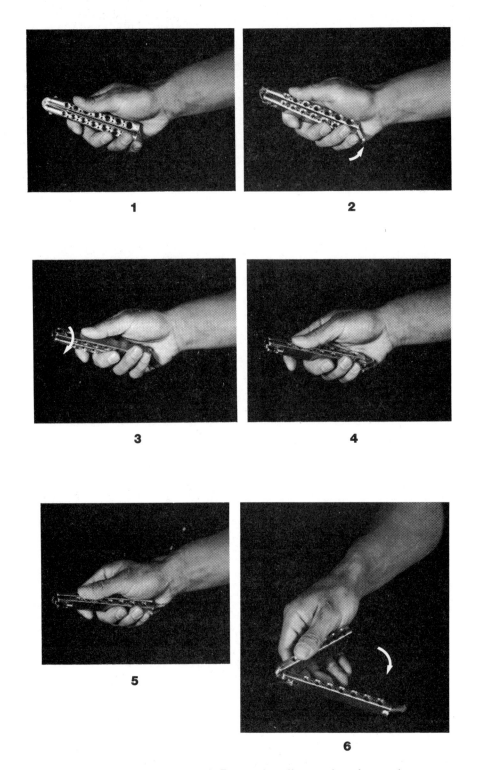

Pop latch with little finger (1 and 2). Rotate handle one-fourth turn (counterclockwise) while retaining "safe" handle (3, 4 and 5). Swing opposing handle out horizontally to the left (6).

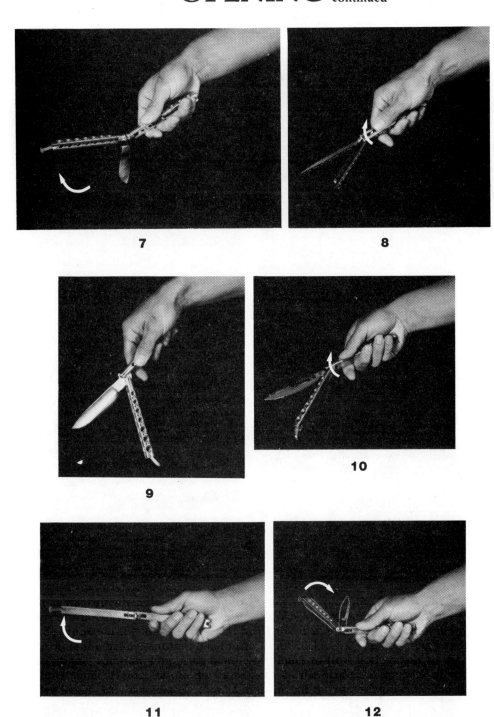

Just as opposing handle swings about 270 degrees, rotate the "safe" handle one-fourth turn (clockwise) with your thumb (8). Your thumb should be over the blade groove in the "safe" handle. When knife is in position similar to photo (9), rotate the handle another one-fourth turn (clockwise). The opposing handle is in continual rotation. Opposing handle continues to flow horizontally to the right (10 and 11). Just before the "safe" side of the blade hits the back of your index finger (12), immediately change direction of the opposing handle and swing it horizontally to the left.

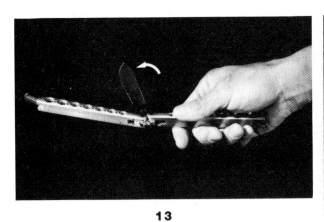

13

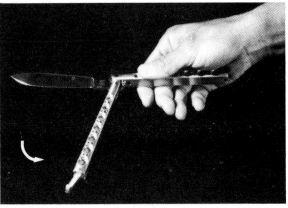

14

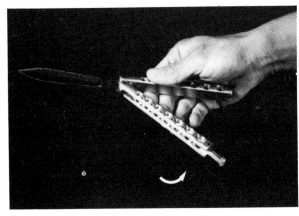

15

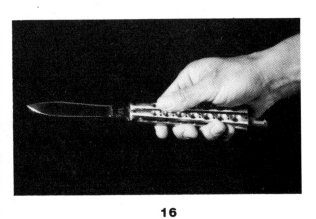

16

As returning handle comes back, prepare your hand to catch it (14, 15 and 16).

HORIZONTAL DOUBLE FLIP CLOSING

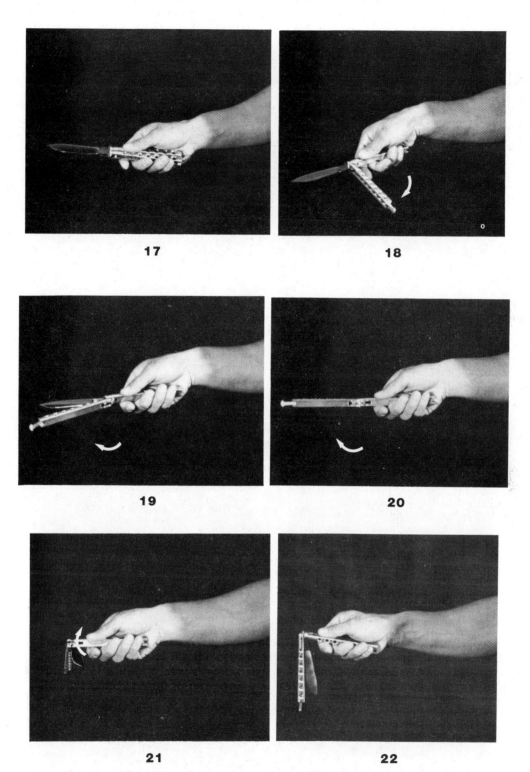

17

18

19

20

21

22

From the horizontal double flip open position (17), prepare to close by holding the "safe" handle and flip the opposing handle horizontally to the left (18). Horizontal motion continues to the right for about 270 degrees (19 and 20). Rotate handle one-fourth turn (clockwise) (21 and 22).

HORIZONTAL DOUBLE FLIP CLOSING

continued

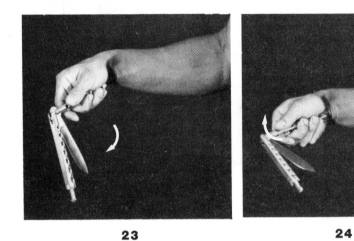

23   **24**

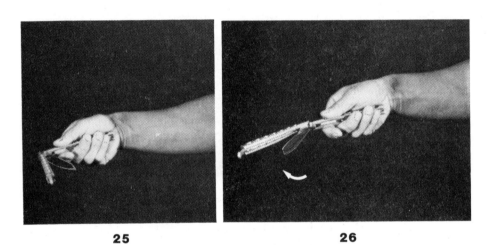

25   **26**

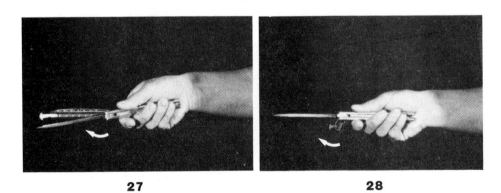

27   **28**

Rotate handle another one-fourth turn (clockwise) (23) and keep blade and handle rotating to the right (24, 25, 26 and 27). Just before the handle hits the back of your index finger (28), pull handle to the left to change direction of the blade.

HORIZONTAL DOUBLE FLIP
CLOSING
continued

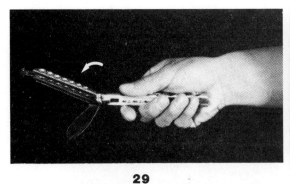

29

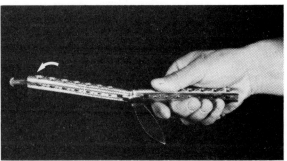

30

31

32

33

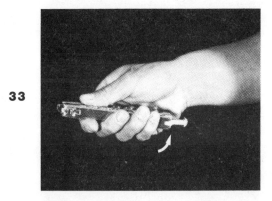

Change direction of blade (29 and 30). Prepare your hand to catch the returning blade and handle into a closed position (31, 32 and 33). Practice the opening and closing together continuously.

HORIZONTAL DOUBLE FLIP
OPENING (latch variation)

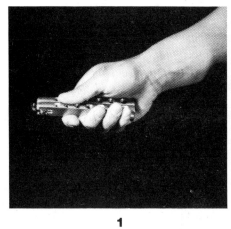

1

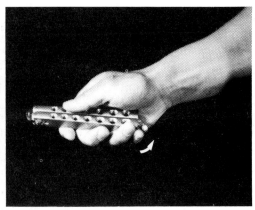

2

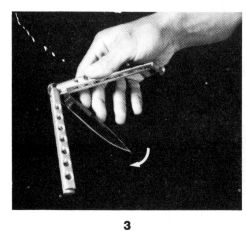

3

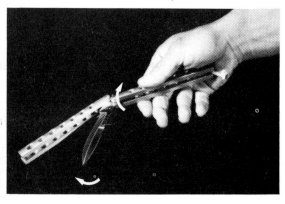

4

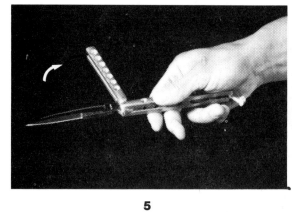

5

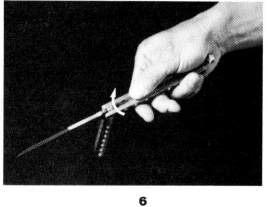

6

HORIZONTAL DOUBLE FLIP
OPENING (latch variation)
continued

7

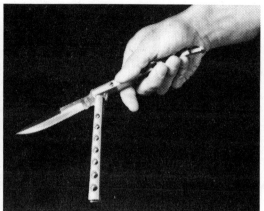

8

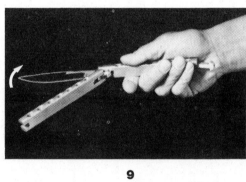

9

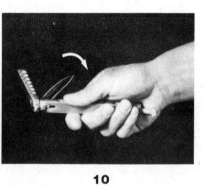

10

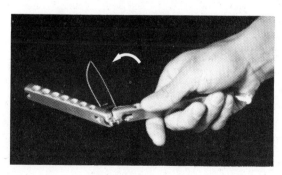

11

HORIZONTAL DOUBLE FLIP
OPENING (latch variation)
continued

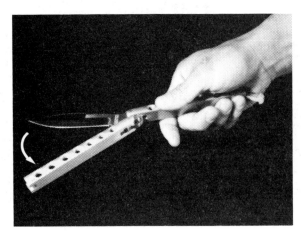

12

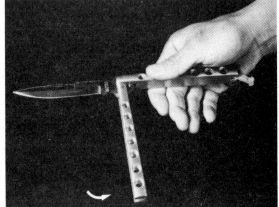

13

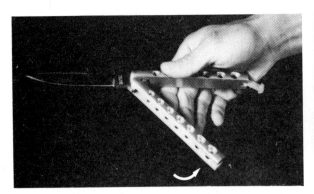

14

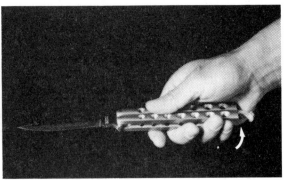

15

This opening is identical to the previous one, except the latch is on the opposite handle.

This is to remind you that the latch doesn't determine which is the "safe" handle. The back side of the blade does.

This is also a modified stiletto or wee hawk blade with half of the upper edge sharpened. In step (10) you must choke up on the handle or pull the blade prior to the back side of the blade striking your index finger or you will definitely get cut.

HORIZONTAL DOUBLE FLIP
OPENING (front view)

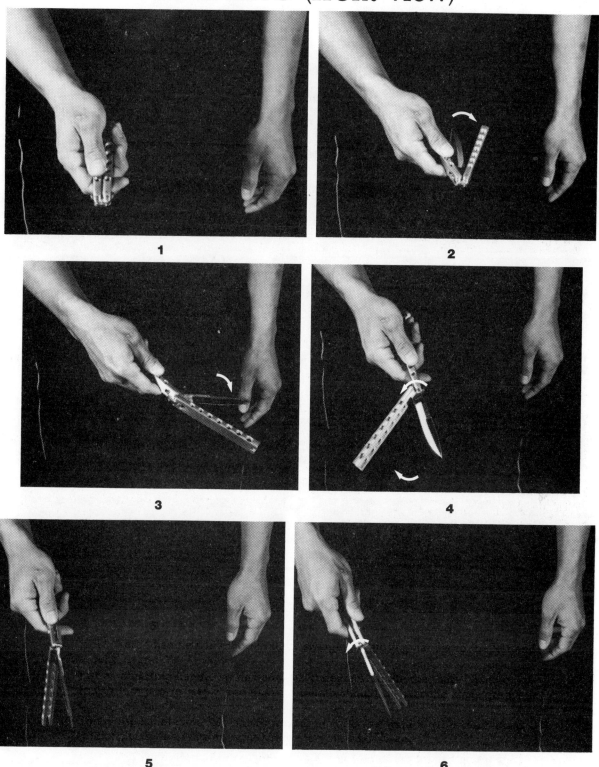

Hold "safe" handle while horizontally swinging opposing handle to the left and around (1 and 2).

Just as opposing handle swings about 270 degrees, rotate the "safe" handle one-fourth turn (clockwise) (3 and 4). Your thumb should be over the blade groove in the "safe" handle (5).

Rotate the handle another one-fourth turn (clockwise) until it is horizontal and continue to swing the opposing handle to your right (6 and 7).

61

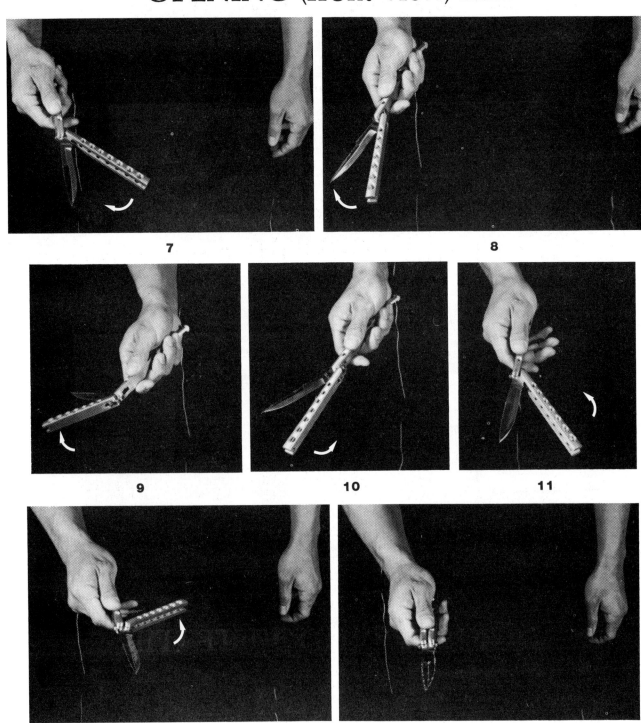

Opposing handle continues to flow horizontally to the right (8).

Just before the back side of the blade strikes the back side of your index finger (9), change blade direction and swing handle and blade to your left (10).

Prepare your hand to accept the returning handle and catch the blade in the open position (11, 12 and 13).

DOUBLE FLIP DOWN OPENING

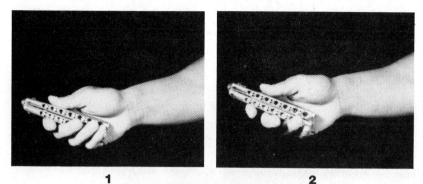

1   **2**

Pop latch open with your little finger (1 and 2).

3

Rotate handle one-fourth turn counterclockwise (3).

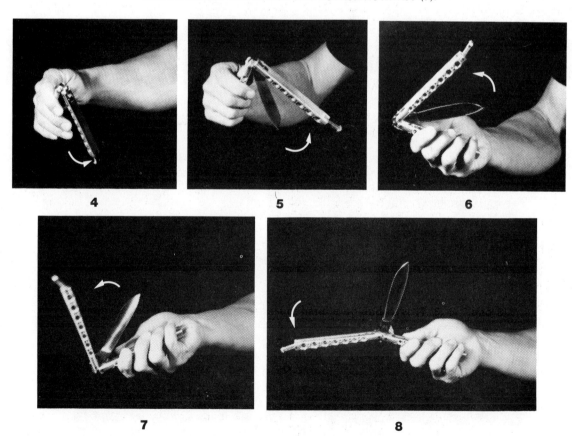

4   **5**   **6**

7   **8**

Retain "safe" handle and flip opposing handle up and over (4, 5, 6, 7 and 8).

DOUBLE FLIP DOWN OPENING
continued

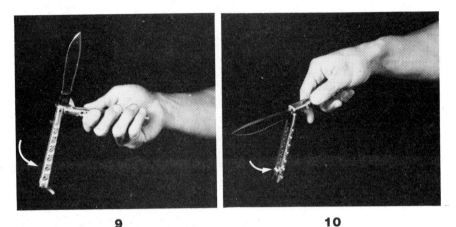

9   10

When handle has traveled about 270 degrees, turn hand counterclockwise (not rotating knife) from a palms up to a palms down position (9 and 10).

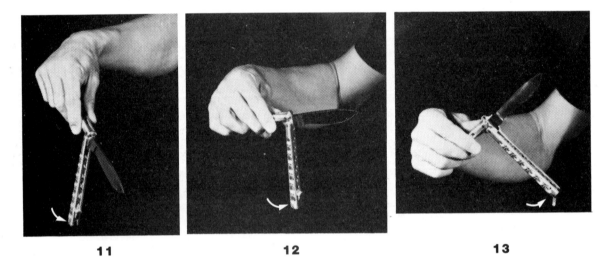

11   12   13

With palm down, flip blade out and over away from you (12 and 13) by turning palm and knife up and over (14, 15, 16 and 17). Just before the safe side of the blade hits the back of your index finger (18), reverse direction of travel (19) and swing knife handle in opposite direction.

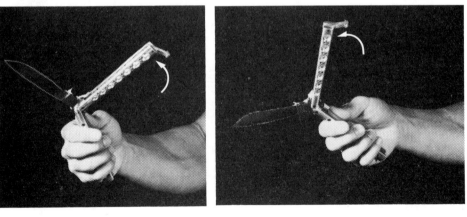

14   15

DOUBLE FLIP DOWN OPENING
continued

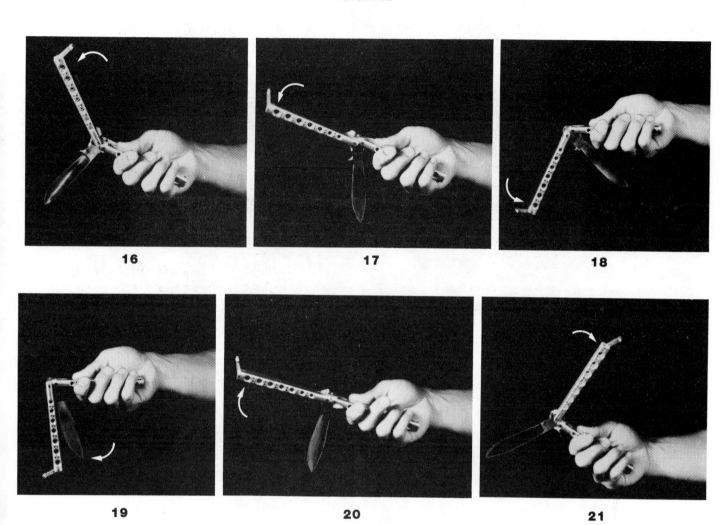

16   17   18

19   20   21

Prepare to catch upcoming handle (20, 21, 22 and 23).

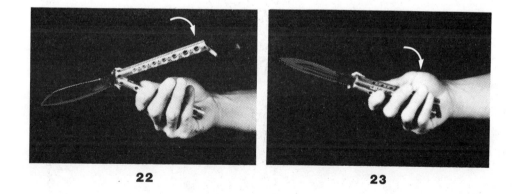

22   23

DOUBLE FLIP DOWN CLOSING

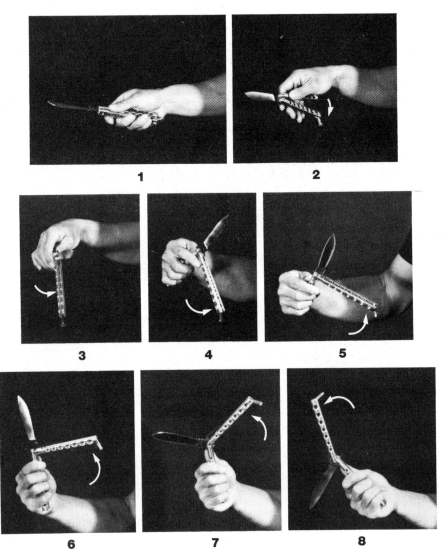

From a sabre grip position (1), retain "safe" handle, turn wrist in, and flip blade up and over, away from your body. This is done by turning your hand from a palm-down position to a palm-up position (2, 3, 4, 5, 6, 7 and 8).

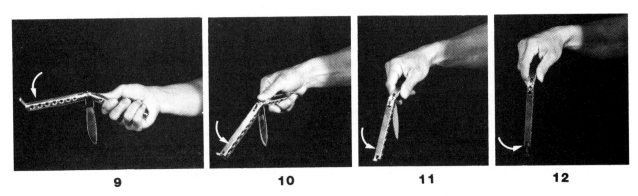

When knife is in position (10), rotate grip (counterclockwise) to a palm-down position without rotating the knife (11 and 12).

DOUBLE FLIP DOWN CLOSING

continued

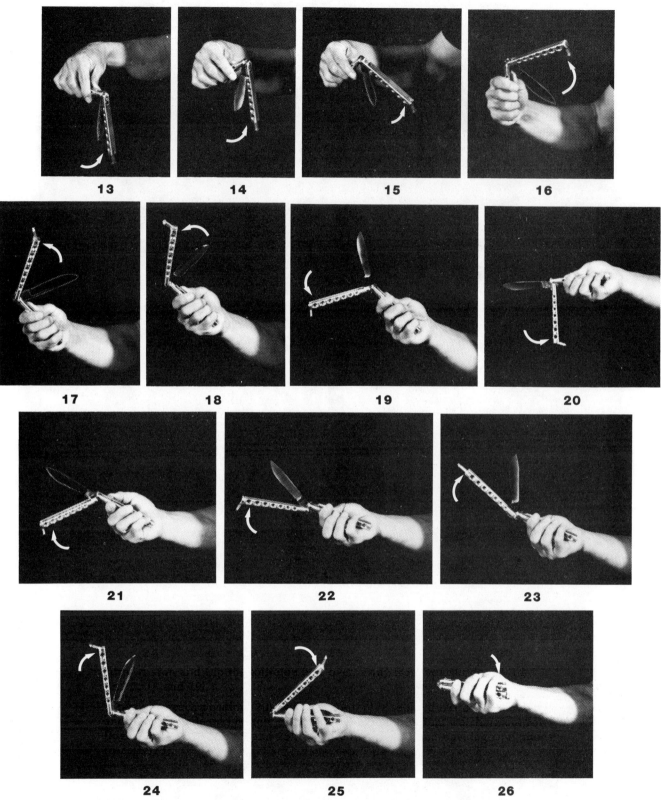

13 **14** **15** **16**

17 **18** **19** **20**

21 **22** **23**

24 **25** **26**

Turn wrist in and flip the knife up and over, away from your body (13, 14, 15, 16, 17, 18 and 19).

When you reach position (20), with palm up, reverse the direction of the swing and flip the blade and handle back into the closed position, watching out for fingers (21, 22, 23, 24, 25 and 26). Practice this closing and opening continuously to perfect it.

67

DOUBLE FLIP DOWN (out to in) OPENING AND CLOSING

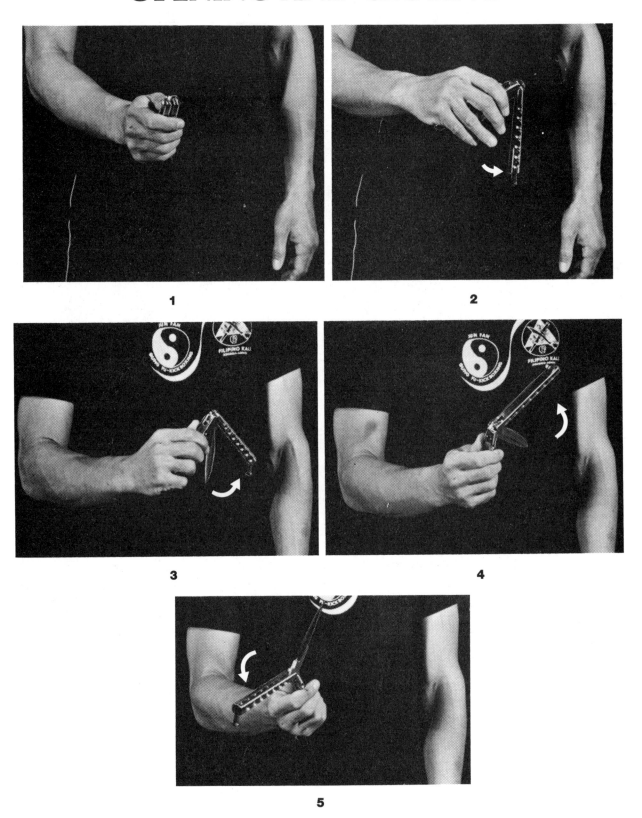

1

2

3

4

5

From starting position (1), retain ''safe'' handle and flip handle up and out, away from your body clockwise (3, 4 and 5).

DOUBLE FLIP DOWN (out to in)
OPENING AND CLOSING
continued

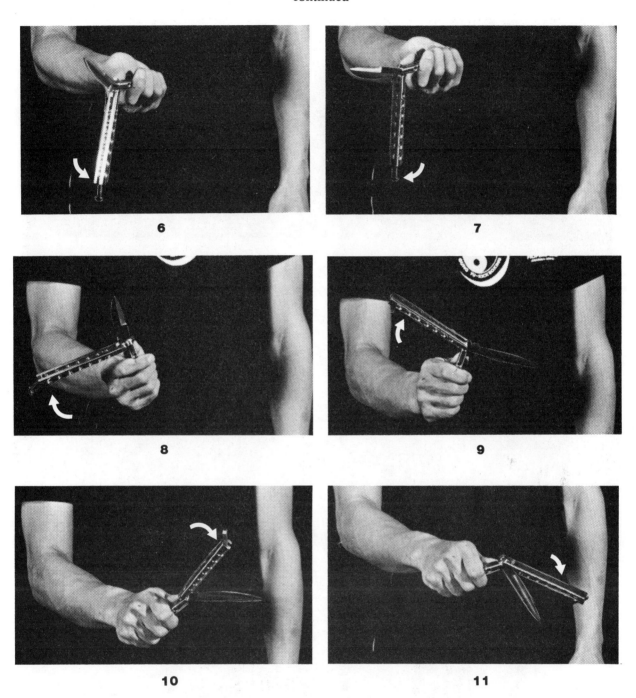

In position (6), change direction and flip knife back in by turning your palm down and counterclockwise (6, 7, 8, 9, 10 and 11).

DOUBLE FLIP DOWN (out to in)
OPENING AND CLOSING
continued

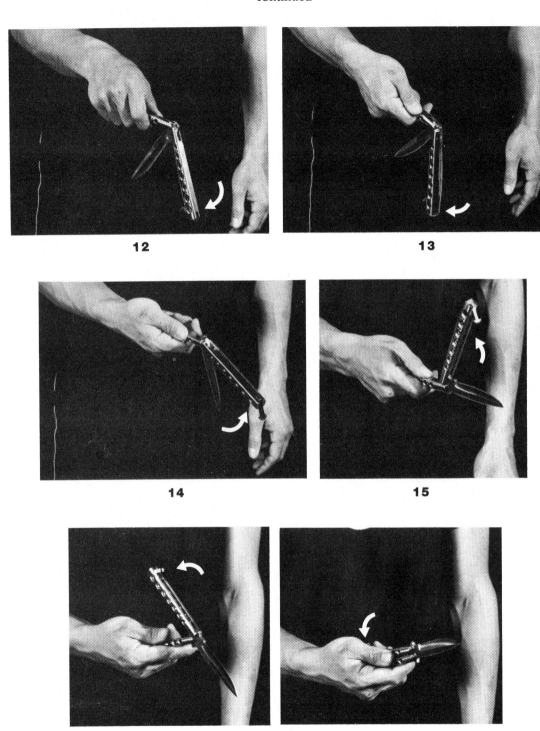

In position (12), rotate grip (don't rotate knife) to a palm-up position (clockwise) (13), and change direction of swing upward toward you (14).

Prepare to catch the upcoming handle (15, 16 and 17).

DOUBLE FLIP DOWN (out to in) OPENING AND CLOSING
continued

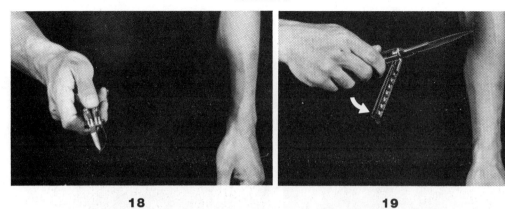

18   **19**

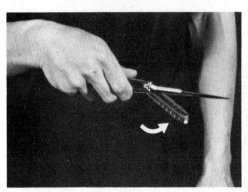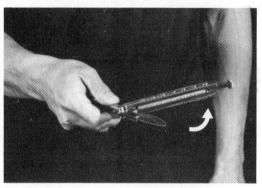

20   **21**

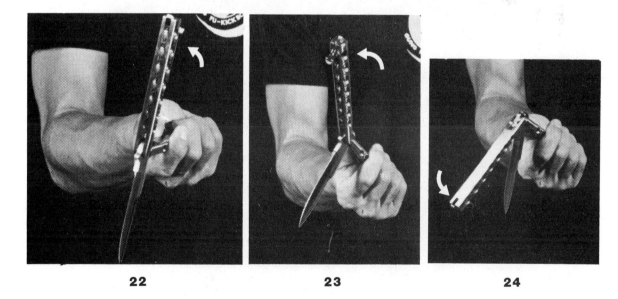

22   **23**   **24**

Go to a horizontal foil grip (18).

Retain "safe" handle and flip knife up and out clockwise (19, 20, 21, 22, 23 and 24).

DOUBLE FLIP DOWN (out to in)
OPENING AND CLOSING
continued

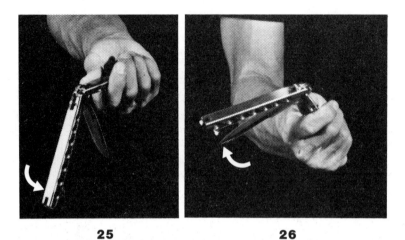

25   26

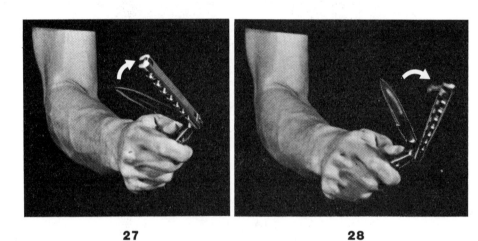

27   28

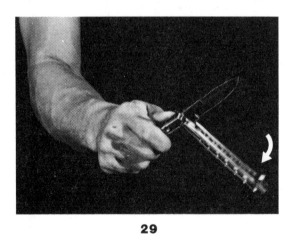

29

Just before the safe side of the blade hits your index finger (25), pull knife to change direction of swing.

Flip your knife back in and down, turning palm down counterclockwise (26, 27, 28 and 29).

DOUBLE FLIP DOWN (out to in)
OPENING AND CLOSING
continued

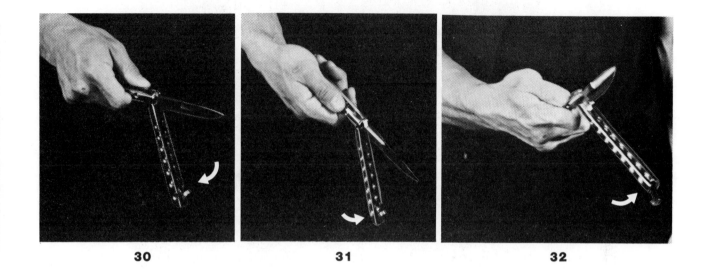

30   31   32

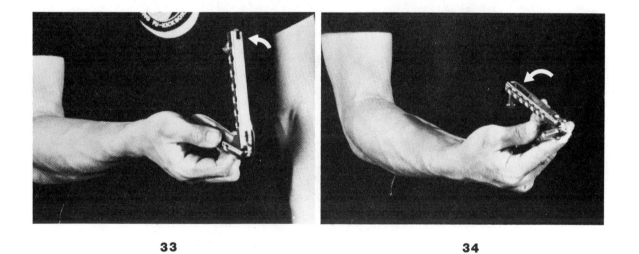

33   34

When knife reaches position (30), rotate your hand only to a palm-up position.

Change direction of the swing by swinging the handle toward you (31).

Prepare for the catch (32, 33 and 34).

SINGLE FLIP OUTSIDE OPENING

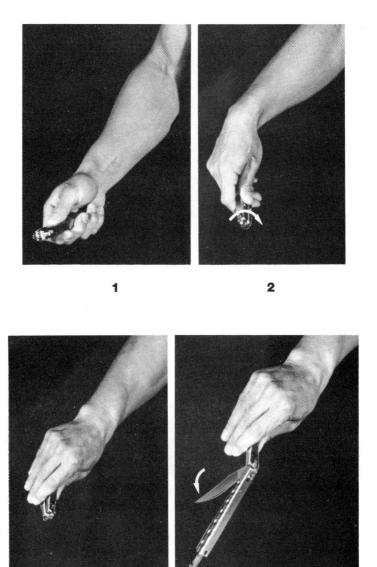

Pop latch with little finger (1).

Rotate wrist one-half turn (counterclockwise) retaining "safe" handle on top (2).

Release and swing opposing handle to outside (3 and 4).

SINGLE FLIP OUTSIDE OPENING
continued

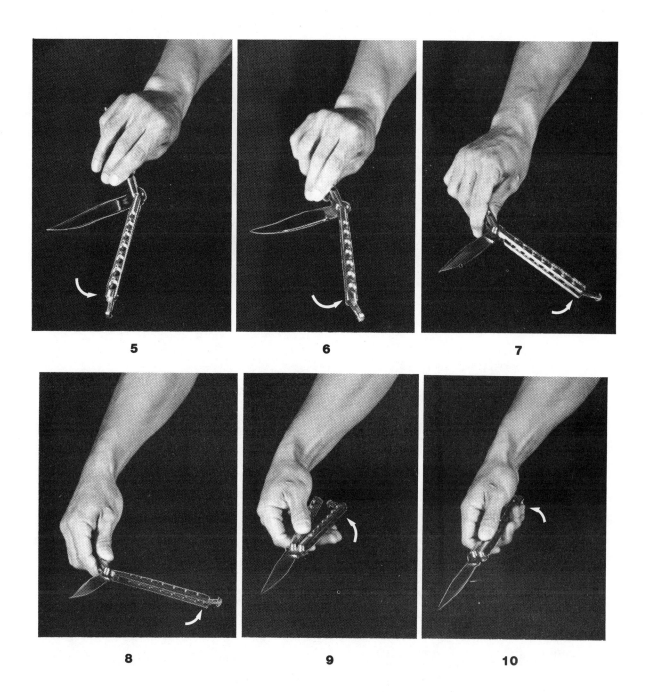

5

6

7

8

9

10

During the counterclockwise swing in steps 5, 6, 7 and 8, the knife grip must be rotated one-half turn to the right.

The handle is already there for you to catch (9), and you end up with a horizontal foil grip (10).

SINGLE FLIP OUTSIDE CLOSING

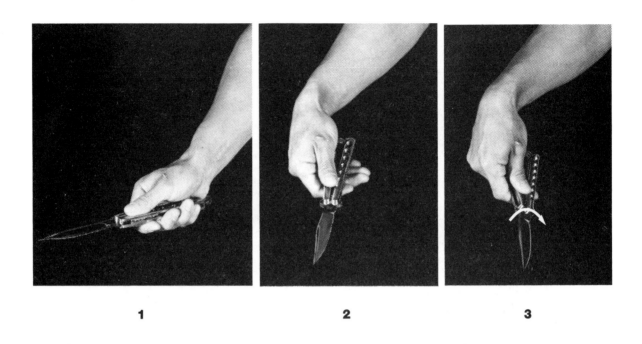

1   2   3

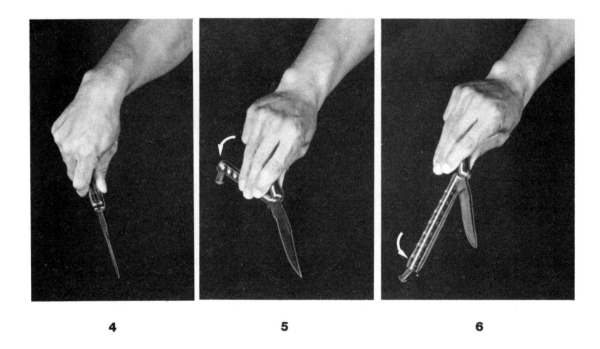

4   5   6

From the horizontal foil grip (1), rotate your hand to a palm-down position (2, 3 and 4).

Retain the "safe" handle, release and swing the opposing handle to outside (5 and 6).

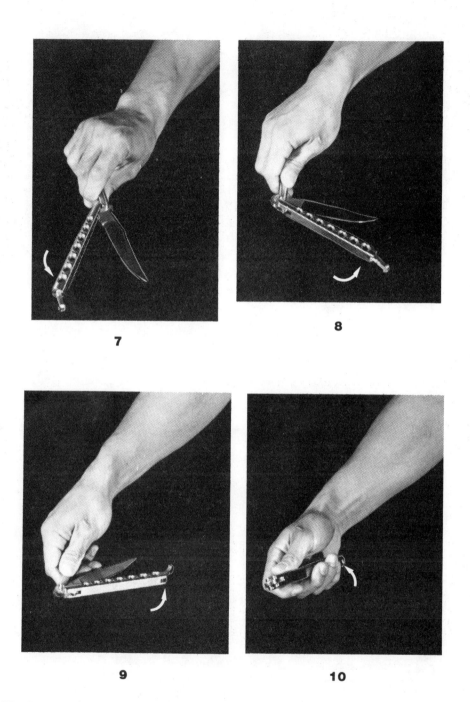

7

8

9

10

The knife will swing counterclockwise and your grip will rotate one-half turn (to the right) to catch the incoming blade and handle (7, 8, 9 and 10).

DOUBLE FLIP HAND EXCHANGE

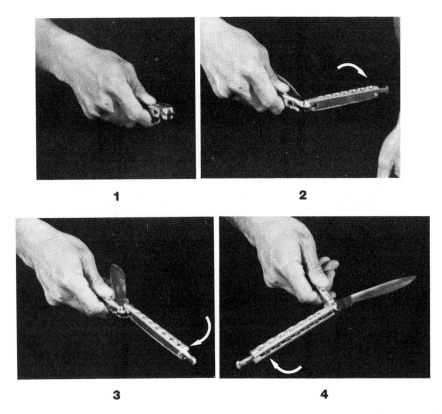

1   2

3   4

Holding the "safe" handle (1), release and swing the opposing handle out to the right (2, 3 and 4).

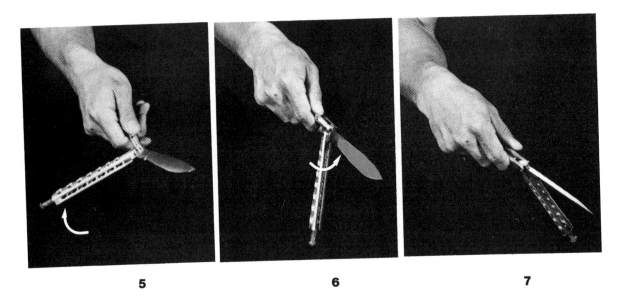

5   6   7

Rotate the handle 180 degrees to your left (5, 6, 7 and 8).

DOUBLE FLIP HAND EXCHANGE

continued

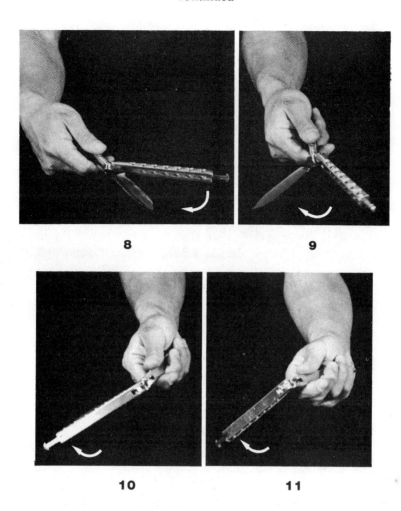

Swing handle to your right (9, 10 and 11).

Just before the safe side of the blade hits your index finger (12), change direction of the handle and swing it to your left.

DOUBLE FLIP HAND EXCHANGE

continued

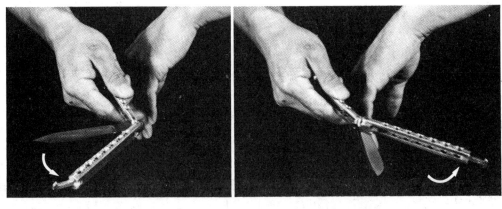

13   14

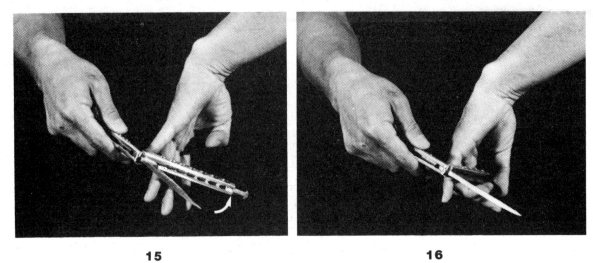

15   16

Have your left hand, in a finger-pointing-down position, ready to catch the incoming handle (13, 14, 15 and 16). Be sure to keep your thumb out of the way.

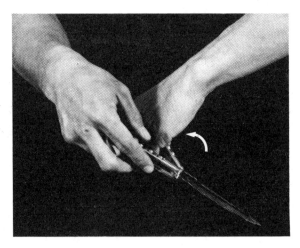

17

Grab the handle with your left hand (17).

DOUBLE FLIP HAND EXCHANGE

continued

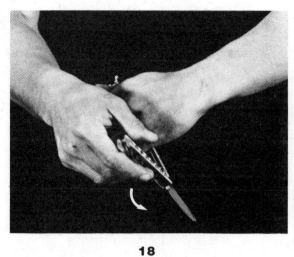

18

19

Release "safe" handle with your right hand and let it drop (18 and 19).

20

21

Pivot knife handle with your left hand 180 degrees, and flip up the "safe" handle into a left-handed, ice-pick grip (20, 21, 22, 23 and 24).

DOUBLE FLIP HAND EXCHANGE

continued

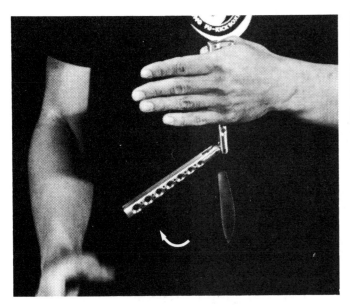

22

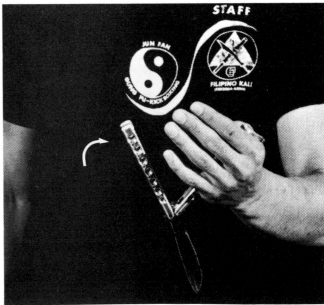

23

We have given you the basic manipulation techniques. Now experiment on your own by changing the angles of the flipping motions. This will open up many variations. Also, experiment with ways to increase your speed, and experiment with a lot of arm motion and limited arm motion. Have fun!

24

WRIST AND FOREARM DRILL

Low wrist twists side to side

Escrima masters use this drill to strengthen their wrists and forearms. Use both hands and all directions, front, back, side, etc.

WRIST AND FOREARM DRILL

High wrist twists side to side

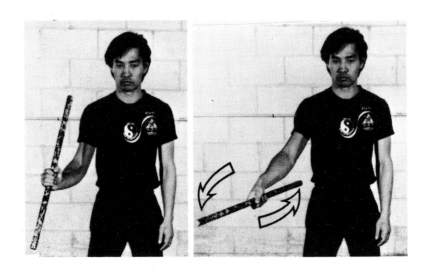

Front wrist snaps

Escrima masters use this drill to strengthen their wrists, arms and shoulders. Use both hands in all directions, front, back, side, etc.

WRIST CIRCLE DRILLS

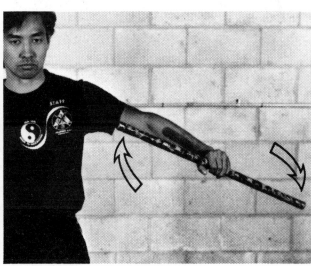

WRIST CIRCLE DRILLS

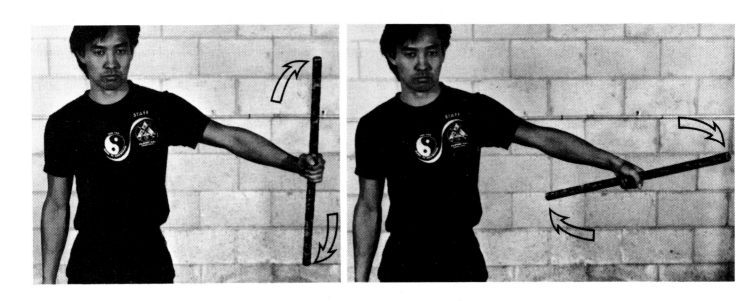

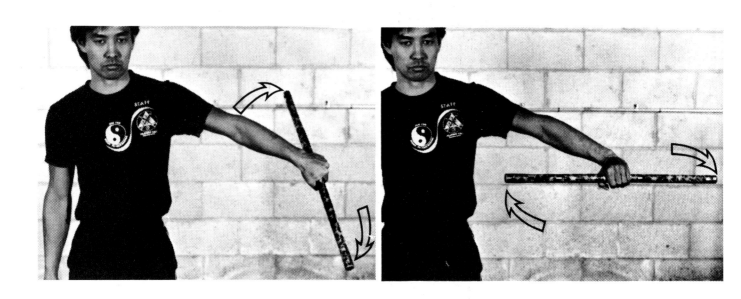

Vary direction and arm location for best results.

FINGER DEXTERITY DRILL

This drill is to promote finger dexterity. Use your fingers to walk the stick down as well as up. You can vary the exercise by holding your arm in different positions.

FINGER GRIP
AND REACTIONS DRILL

Select various objects, drop them, and catch them with alternating fingers. For reaction times, drop the object, throw a punch or kick, and then catch the falling object.

GRIP CHANGING DRILL

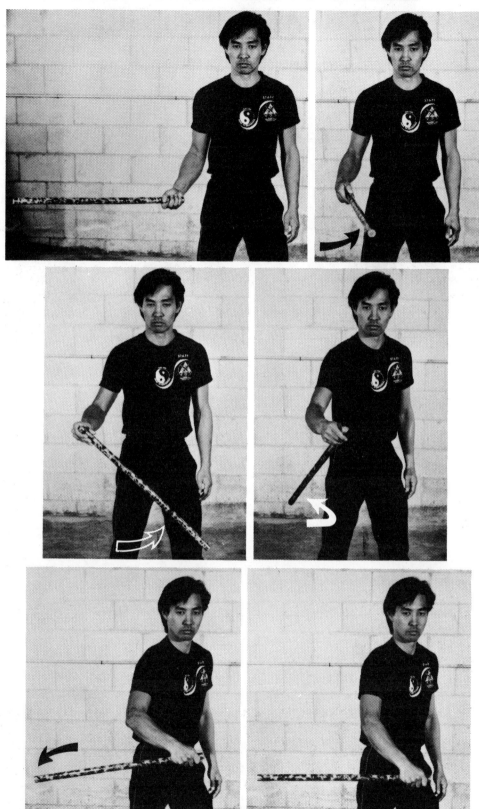

This drill or exercise is performed with a 24-inch Filipino escrima stick. It will help you visualize one of the grip changes you can do with a knife, and it is a good exercise to strengthen your hands, fingers, wrists and forearms. Use a heavy stick for strength and a lighter stick to enhance your speed, dexterity and agility.

STICK/KNIFE MOTION
COMPARISON DRILL

This drill will further help you visualize the hand and arm motions involved during manipulation. For best results, alternate the knife and stick for each hand.

 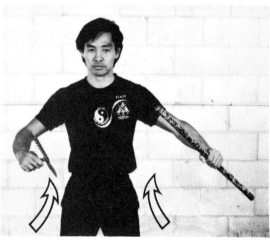

STICK/KNIFE MOTION
COMPARISON DRILL
continued

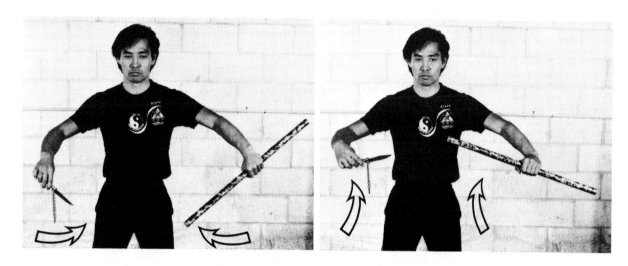

SELF-DEFENSE
WITH THE BALISONG

Any sensible person will avoid a fight if given the choice. However, under many circumstances you are not always allowed to make that choice. The aim, then, is to prepare for a fight as much as it is to avoid one. Knowing how to fight raises your awareness about when trouble is coming, which is truly an art in itself. Bruce Lee emphasized this in "Enter the Dragon" when he stated that his style was not a style, but an art—"the art of fighting without fighting."

Self defense is the right to protect yourself against violence or threatened violence with whatever means are *reasonably* necessary. The highest level of self defense is to stop or avoid an act of violence before it starts.

The second level is to immediately neutralize an attack with as little force as is necessary. And the third level is to use as much force as is required to gain control of the situation. A defense that inflicts more violence than is required is not legally or morally acceptable and makes you no better than the attacker.

Attacks take place when the attacker assumes you are unable or unwilling to defend yourself. Attackers choose those who they expect to behave as a helpless or passive victim or who they want to intimidate. Bullies who attack and find they don't have a willing or helpless victim are often discouraged.

The balisong knife is a very moral self-defense tool, because of its yin and yang qualities. It has a peaceful mode as well as a violent one, whereas, once drawn, a regular knife is solely a tool of maximum force. The balisong can be used in stages and degrees depending on your needs.

In the peaceful or nonaggressive mode, it can be used like a Japanese yawara or Filipino tabak maliit (pocket stick). Yet, with a slight change of wrist movement, it conveniently and rapidly converts from a defensive to an offensive weapon.

Please don't misinterpret this section as encouraging you to challenge a knife fighter. Avoiding any confrontation is still the best defense. The following situations are merely examples and are by no means the only solutions.

1

2

3

4

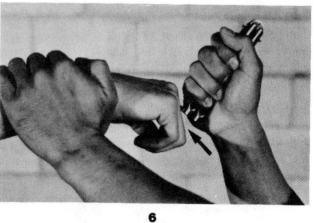

5

6

This sequence illustrates a quick way to stop or discourage an attacker from throwing a punch at you. Step back just enough to avoid the right cross (3). Hand check and grab the incoming punch (4 and 5), and smash the knuckles or hand with the butt of the balisong (6). The pain should convince the attacker that a serious defense is intended.

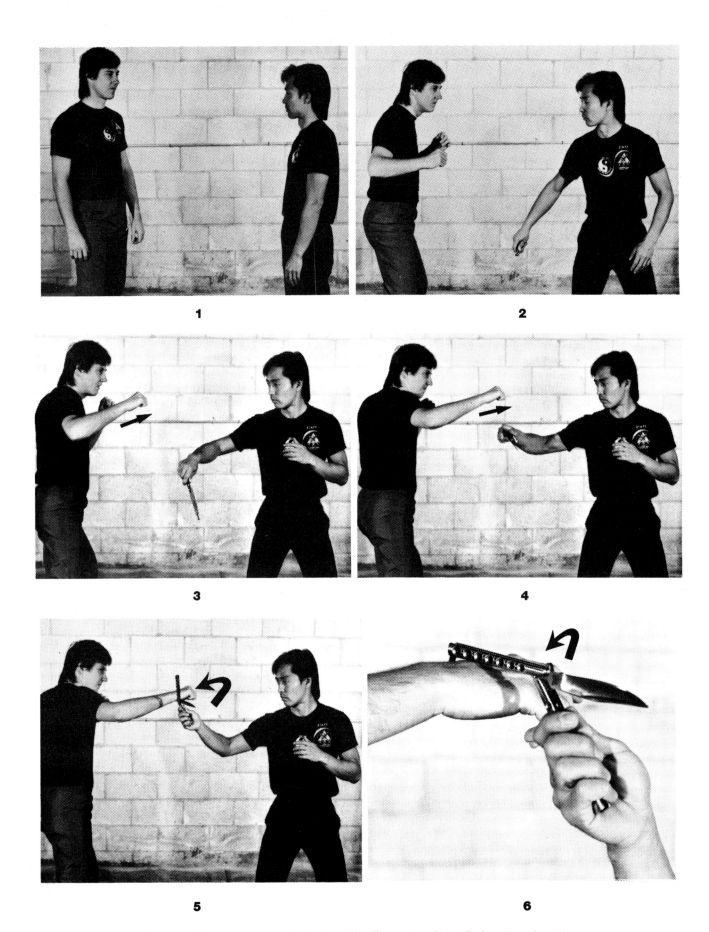

1

2

3

4

5

6

This is a flailing stop hit (2, 3, 4 and 5). The pain of the flailing hit plus the knowledge that you possess a weapon will put a stop to further aggressive action.

1

2

3

4

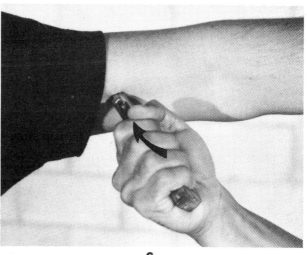

5

6

This defensive sequence requires a little more martial arts training since your distance and timing are critical.

Step back to avoid his left jab (3). Hand check his punch with your left hand (4). While controlling his hand, immediately strike the bicep with the tang of the balisong (5).

95

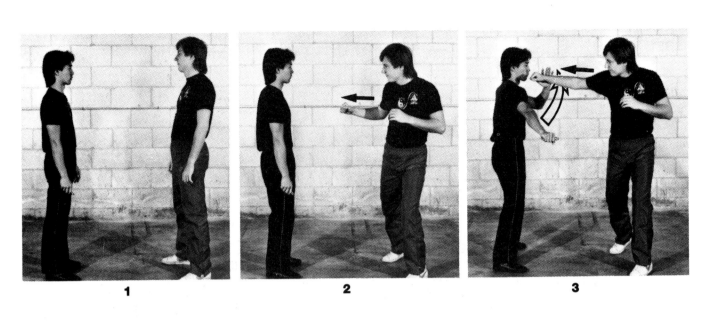

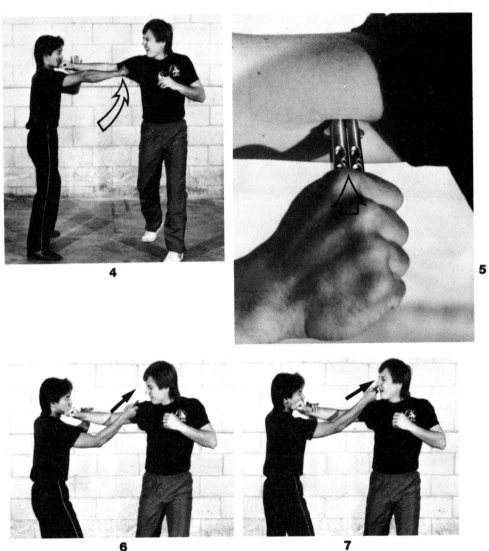

This defense is similar to the previous technique. The attacker throws a right jab to your face (2), angle to your left and hand check his right with your left (3). Strike to the inner bicep with the balisong tang (5) and in one continuous motion go to the face (7).

1

2

3

4

5

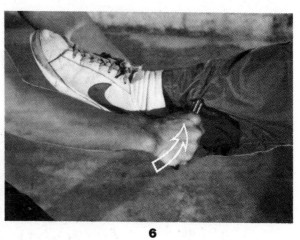

6

As the attacker throws a right, front snap-kick, step back and angle away from the kick (3). Use your left hand to check and control his leg (4), and immediately strike his shin or ankle with the tang of the balisong (5). Notice we are always striking sensitive parts of the body to dispatch the attack as efficiently and effortlessly as possible.

97

1   2

3   4   continued

Train yourself to be aware and to prevent anyone from sneaking up on you from behind. In step (2), you can immediately strike to the groin with your right hand, but in this scenario, he might be a friend, so you let the pressure of the body grab tell you whether he is friend or foe.

If foe, simultaneously place your left hand under his grab and prepare to strike the back of his hand with the butt of your balisong (3). This is a very sensitive area and should result in a quick release (4).

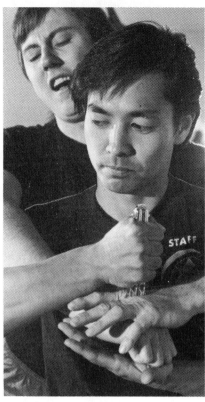

5

6

7

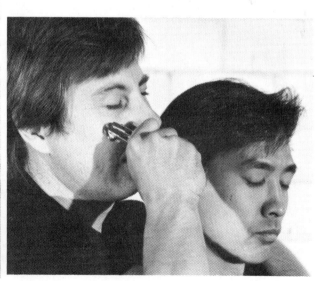

8

You can take it further by sandwiching his trapped hands, and grinding into that area with the closed balisong (5).

If he has a high pain tolerance and is still holding on, move your left hand on top of his to prevent him from going to a choke and strike to the face with the tang of the balisong (7 and 8).

1

2

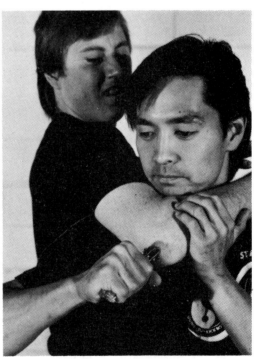

3

4

Your attacker has a choke hold on you, so grab his right arm with your left hand
(1). Turn your head to the bend in his arm to prevent your Adam's apple from
getting smashed or your windpipe from being blocked (2). Immediately strike his
right elbow with the tang or butt of the balisong (3 and 4).

100

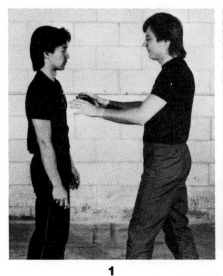
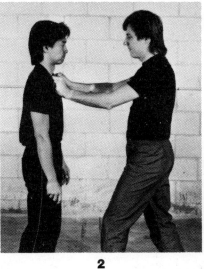

1 **2** **3**

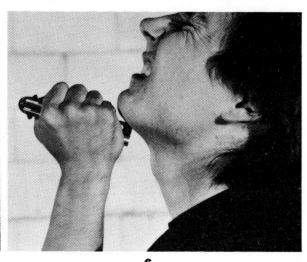

4 **5** **6**

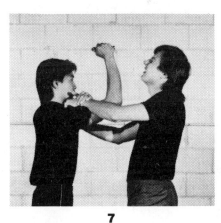
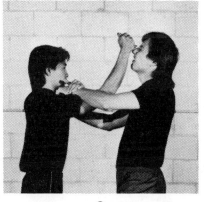

7 **8**

Your attacker comes in with a double-hand, front-lunge grab (1 and 2). If you can't avoid the grab, quickly place your left hand and arm over the top of his hands to prevent him from going to your throat and to redirect his energy (3). Your right hand and balisong comes straight up to a chin or neck strike (4, 5 and 6). Follow through from the upward strike and come down with a nose bridge or face strike (7 and 8).

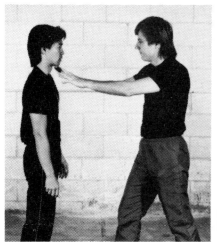

1   **2**   **3**

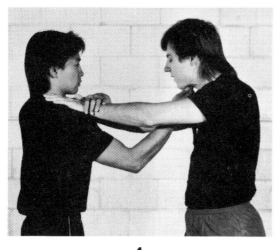

4

5

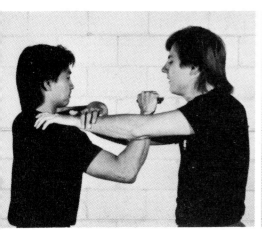
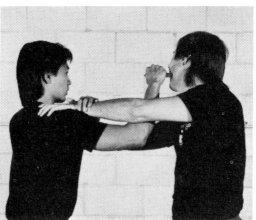
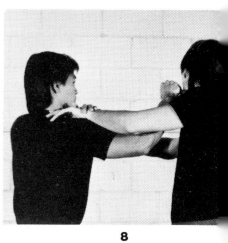

6   **7**   **8**

This defense sequence is similar to the previous one, only using different parts
of the weapon (5), and different strikes (6, 7 and 8). Always look at the root of
the technique and use whatever fits, flows or works.

102

1

2

3

4

5

6

7

A person coming at you with a drawn knife could feel quite confident. Pulling a balisong and manipulating it could psychologically undermine an inexperienced attacker. He doesn't know your proficiency, and this mystique can be drawn upon to gain a psychological advantage over him. If you can convince him that you are now the aggressor and that you have every intention of dispatching him in a most unpleasant manner, the conflict should end without any bloodshed.

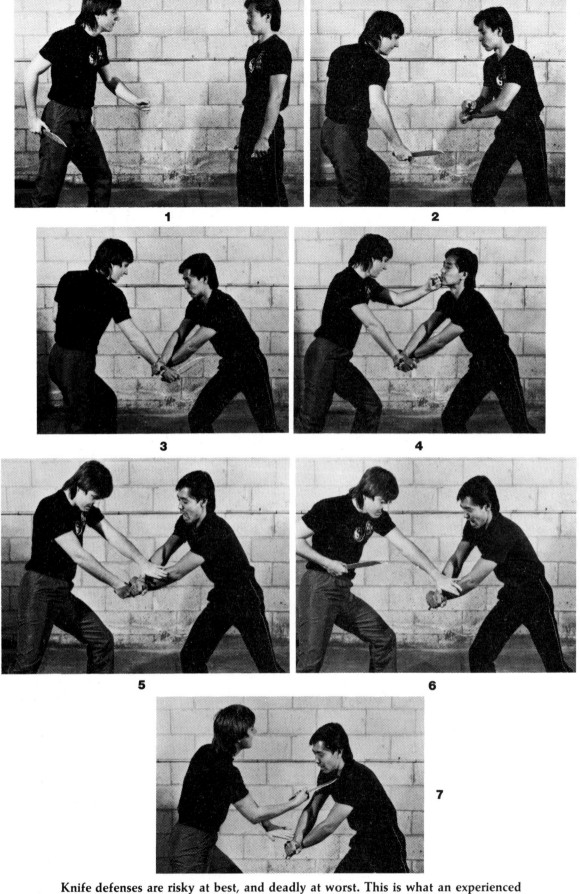

Knife defenses are risky at best, and deadly at worst. This is what an experienced Filipino knife fighter can do against a typical cross-block defense.

The defender tries to block the underhanded midsection thrust with a cross block (3). The weakness of this defense is that both of your hands are tied up or occupied. The attacker can distract you with a punch (4), trap your hands (5) and slice your wrist and hands by merely pulling his knife back (6), and go to the jugular for effect (7).

104

A SAFER SOLUTION

If you can't avoid the confrontation, a better solution would be to angle away from the thrust (3), hit and parry the thrusting hand staying away from the blade (4), strike the right bicep (5), and follow up with an eye jab while always maintaining control of the knife hand (6 and 7).

1

2

3

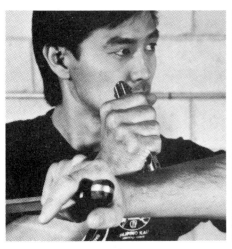

4

5

6

7

8

9

This sequence shows another nonlethal counter to a knife attack using two closed balisongs. The attacker throws an upper body jab (2). Angle away from the thrust, hit and check the attacker's right hand while simultaneously striking to his eyes with your left hand (3). This can be followed up with three more hits to the blinded attacker (6, 7, 8 and 9). Note that you are always in control of his knife-wielding hand.

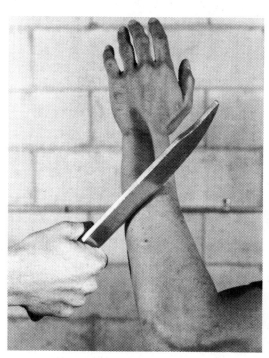 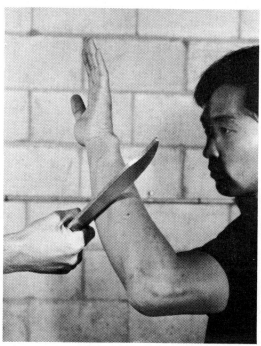

A fact of life in knife fighting is that you must be able to take a cut, because you will be cut. It is often necessary to sacrifice to gain an advantage. You must know anatomy so that you know what area of your own body to protect, as well as the most vulnerable area of your opponent's body to attack.

Realize that any sacrifice you take must immediately be followed up with a destructive blow to your attacker or else the sacrifice is wasted. Besides, taking a blow will only encourage your attacker to finish you off, much like a boxer going after a staggered opponent or an animal stalking his injured prey.

If you have to take a cut on the arm, for example, take it on the outside (left photo), and not on the inside (right photo), where all your veins and arteries are located.

Here are some serious facts to consider: A cut to the brachial artery will result in loss of consciousness in 13 to 15 seconds and death in one a half minutes. A cut to the radial artery will result in loss of consciousness in 30 seconds and death in two minutes.

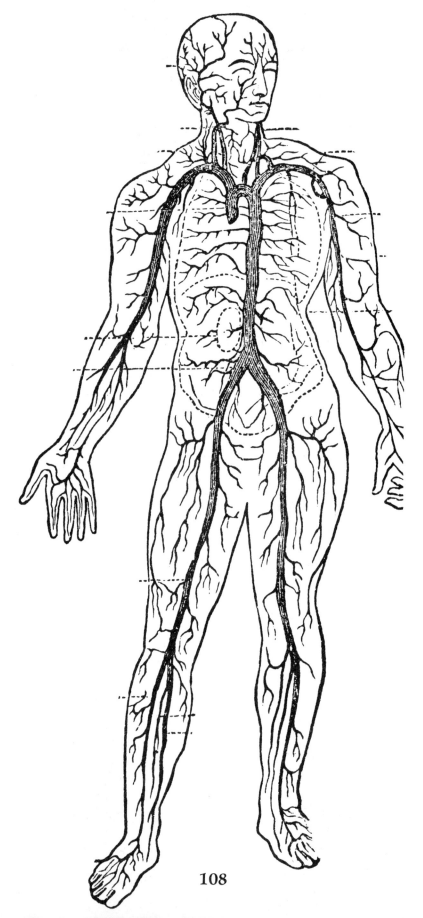

The proper way to block a thrust.

1

2

3

1

2

3

The wrong way.

1   2

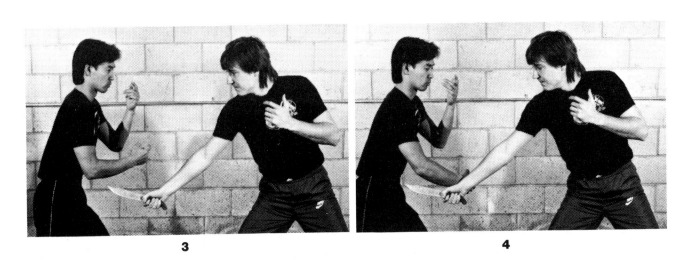

3   4

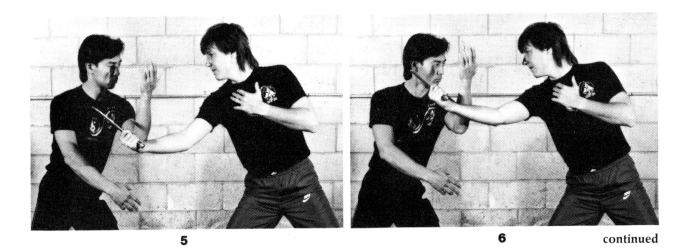

5   6   continued

These three pages of photos show a typical Filipino knife-fighting exercise for in-fighting. Notice the correct parries, hand checks, movements to avoid the blade, and the right moment to perform your own attack. This only comes from practice, instincts and feel.

7

8

9

10

11

12   continued

111

13

14

15

16

17

18

Up to this point we have yet to unshield the blade in a combative situation. It would not do justice to the unique design of the balisong if we didn't. But, all of the following techniques are cut short once the blade is uncovered, because it is not our intention to show you how to maim, disable or kill. We do this out of respect to all the Filipino masters who have preserved and protected this art so well for 900 years.

1

2

3

4

continued

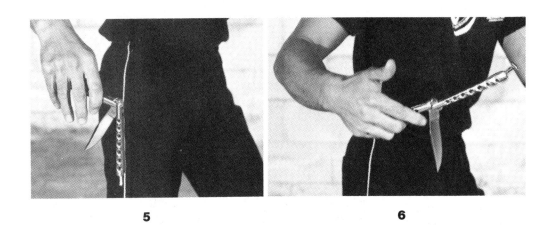

5   6

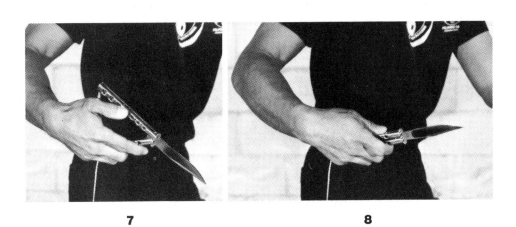

7   8

9   10

One simple counter to a cross-draw knife attack is to angle away (3) and control the elbow of your attacker (4), while simultaneously opening your balisong to keep your attacker at bay. This is a reverse upward knife opening. Constant practice with the balisong will allow you to control it unconsciously, and enable you to focus only on the offensive moves of your attacker.

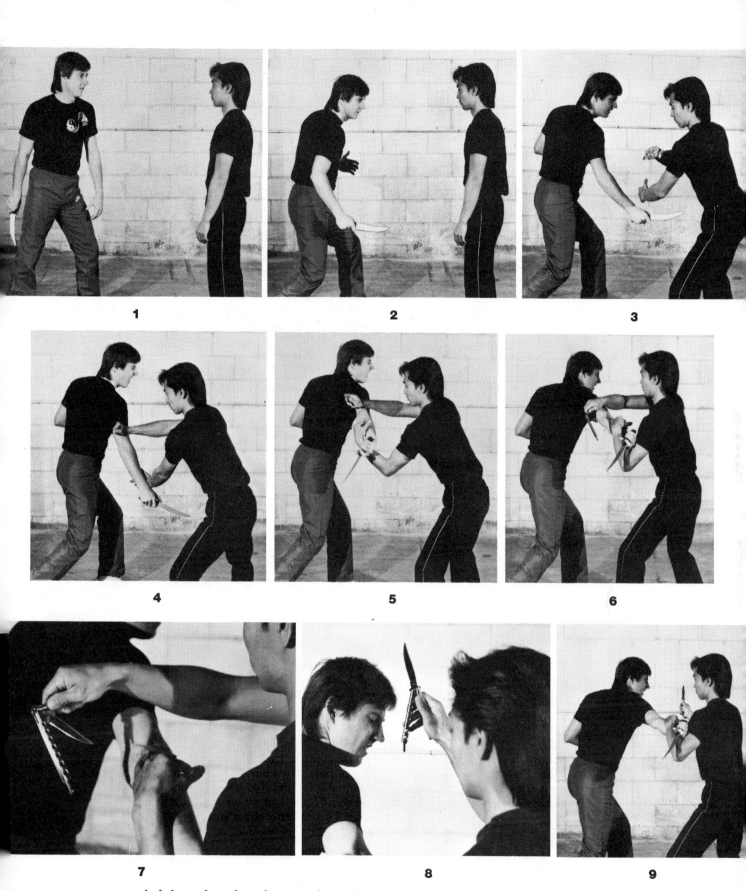

1

2

3

4

5

6

7

8

9

A defense for a low thrust to the midsection (2) calls for avoiding the thrust (3), a left-hand check to the knife hand and a simultaneous hit to the back of the bicep with a closed balisong (4). The painful bicep distraction allows you to perform a wrist/elbow lock (6). The opening of the balisong will show your attacker that any further resistance is futile (7 and 8).

115

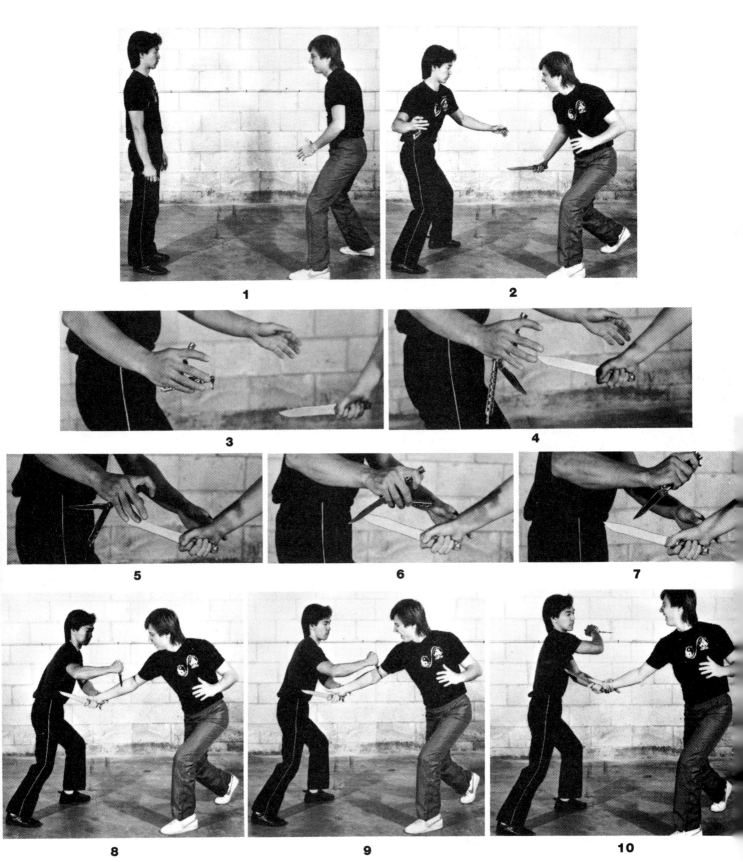

Your attacker leaves you no time or room for a peaceful defensive maneuver (2). Immediately, open your balisong with an ice pick drop catch (3, 4, 5, 6 and 7), and simultaneously hand check and evade the incoming body thrust (8). A slash to the arm may be necessary to halt the confrontation. Quoting Bruce Lee: ''Let your opponent graze your skin and you smash into his flesh; let him smash into your flesh and you fracture his bones; let him fracture your bones and you take his life!''

116

This is a similar defense for an upper-body attack.

117

Without an opponent, let's review the many striking modes available with the balisong.

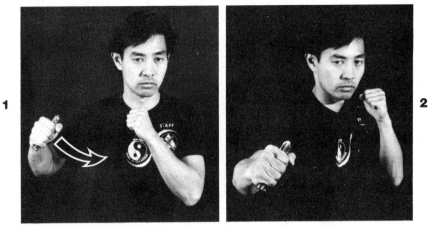

A right hook with a loaded-fist balisong.

A right jab with a loaded-fist balisong.

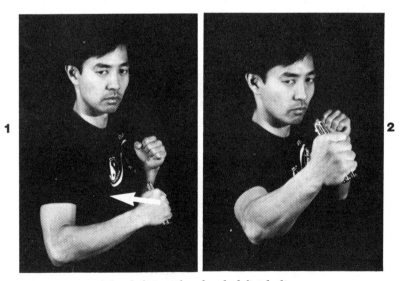

A back-fist with a loaded-fist balisong.

1

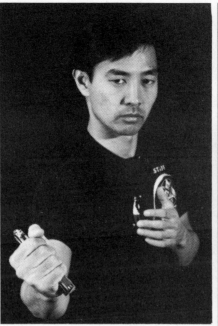

2

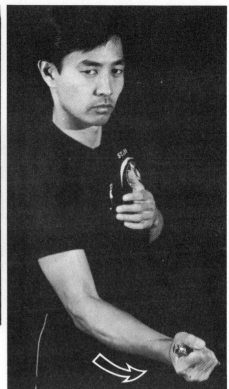

3

All of the following types of attacks originate from the Filipino Number 1 angle. There are 11 other basic angles of attack so, as you can see, the possible combinations are endless. The balisong used like a tabak maliit or yawara, with a hammer-fist butt strike (above).

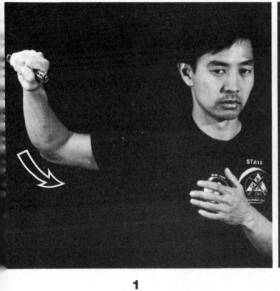

1

2

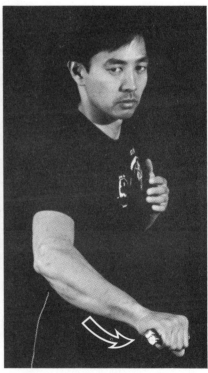

3

An overhead tang strike.

119

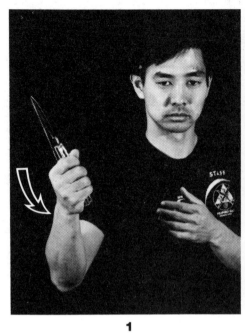
1

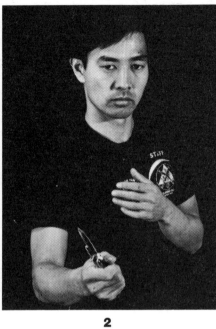
2

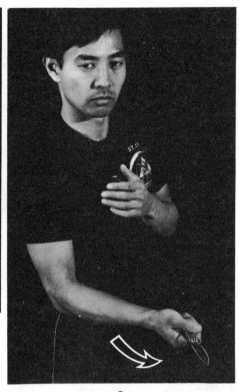
3

A diagonal downward slash.

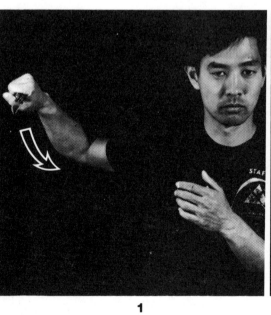
1

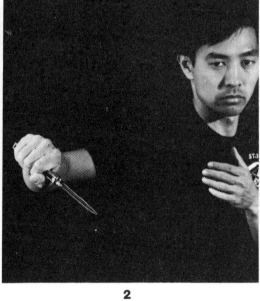
2

3

A diagonal downward thrust.

1

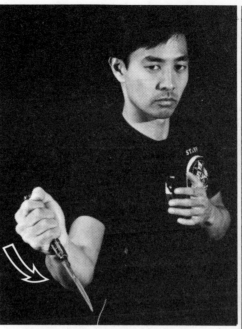

2

3

An ice pick downward thrust.

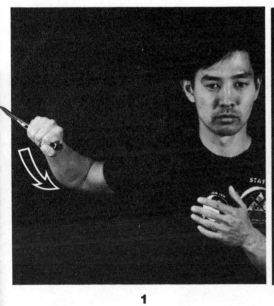

1

2

3

A reverse ice pick downward slash.

121

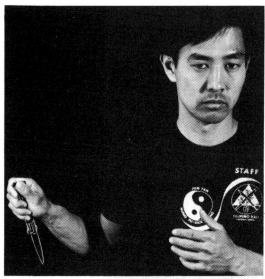

1

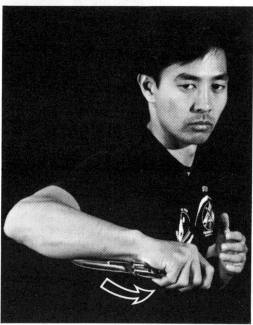

2

3

A reverse ice pick concealed slash.

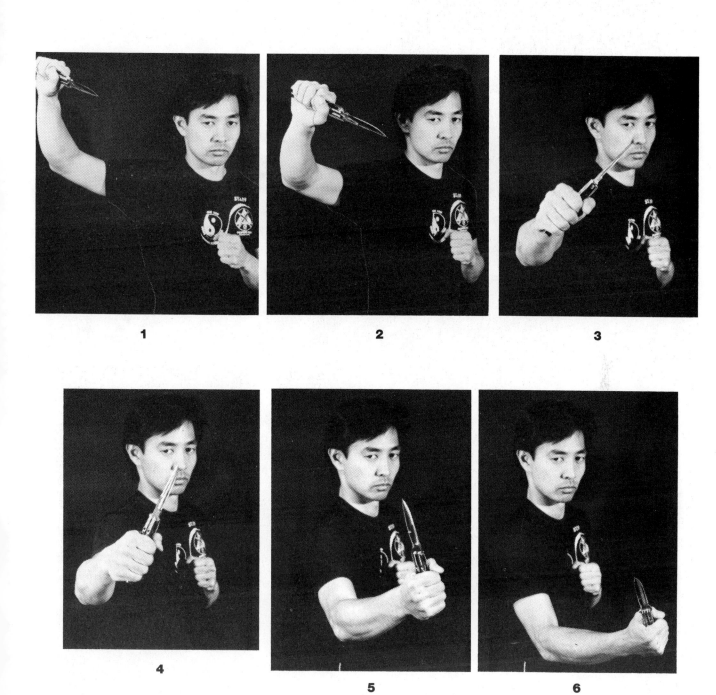

1

2

3

4

5

6

These are more advanced strike combinations, which are almost impossible to counter—the hatchet thrust and slash.

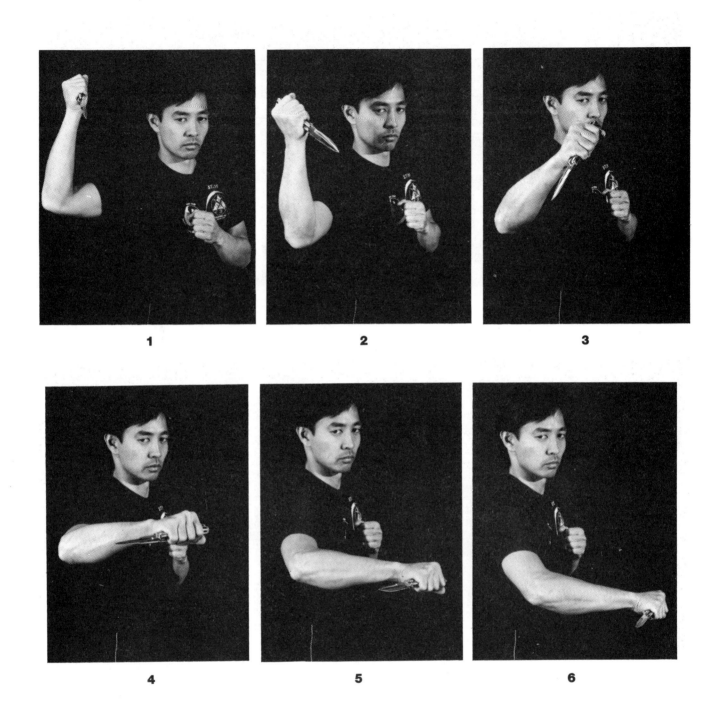

1   2   3

4   5   6

The reverse ice pick thrust and slash.

124

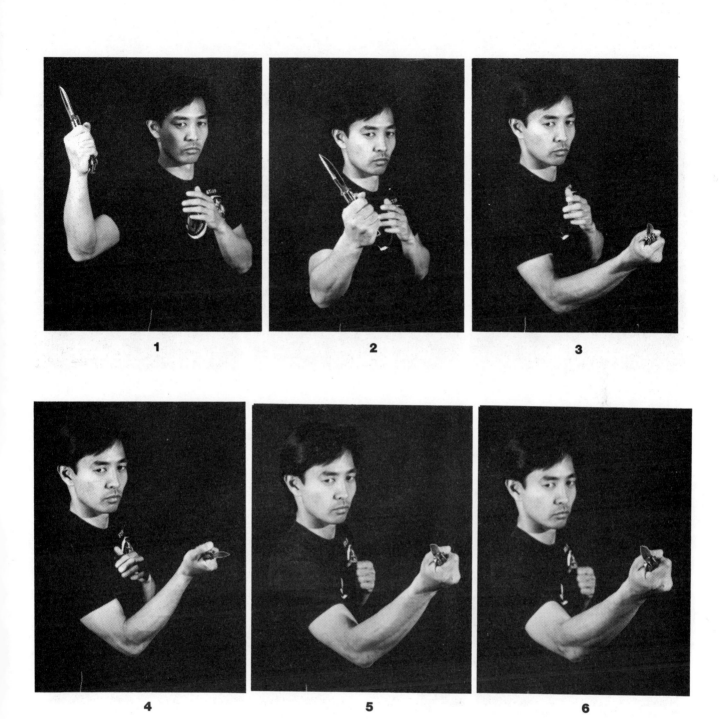

The hatchet grip slash and forward thrust.

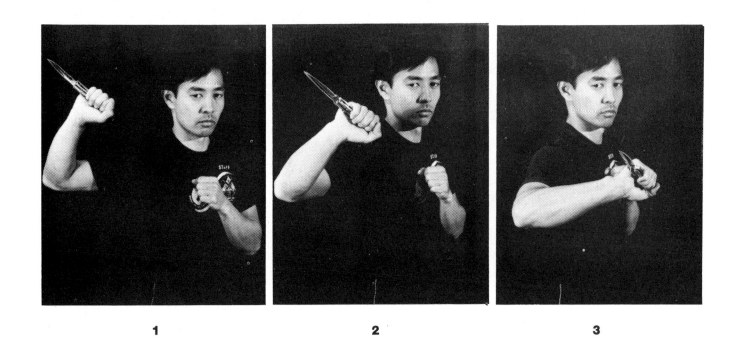

1   2   3

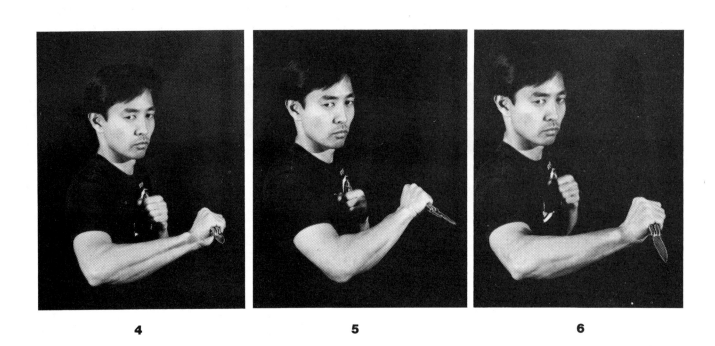

4   5   6

The reverse ice pick slash and backhand thrust.

BALISONG OWNERSHIP RECORD

Date Purchased	Description	Cost	Remarks